PSYCHOLOGY PRACTITIONER GUIDEBOOKS

EDITORS

Arnold P. Goldstein, Syracuse University
Leonard Krasner, Stanford University & SUNY at Stony Brook
Sol L. Garfield, Washington University in St. Louis

TREATMENT OF RAPE VICTIMS

Pergamon Titles of Related Interest

Bart/O'Brien STOPPING RAPE: Successful Survival Strategies

Becker/Heimberg/Bellack SOCIAL SKILLS TRAINING TREATMENT FOR DEPRESSION

Blechman/Brownell HANDBOOK OF BEHAVIORAL MEDICINE FOR WOMEN

Brassard/Germain/Hart PSYCHOLOGICAL MALTREATMENT OF CHILDREN AND YOUTH

Goldstein/Keller AGGRESSIVE BEHAVIOR: Assessment and Intervention

Gotlib/Colby TREATMENT OF DEPRESSION: An Interpersonal Systems Approach

Mrazek/Kempe SEXUALLY ABUSED CHILDREN AND THEIR FAMILIES

Saigh POSTTRAUMATIC STRESS DISORDER: A Behavioral Approach to Assessment and Treatment

Walker/Bonner/Kaufman THE PHYSICALLY AND SEXUALLY ABUSED CHILD: Evaluation and Treatment

Related Journals
(Free sample copies available upon request)

CHILD ABUSE AND NEGLECT
CHILDREN AND YOUTH SERVICES REVIEW
CLINICAL PSYCHOLOGY REVIEW
WOMEN'S STUDIES INTERNATIONAL FORUM

TREATMENT OF RAPE VICTIMS

Facilitating Psychosocial Adjustment

KAREN S. CALHOUN
University of Georgia

BEVERLY M. ATKESON
Florida State University

PERGAMON PRESS
Member of Maxwell Macmillan Pergamon Publishing Corporation
New York • Oxford • Beijing • Frankfurt
São Paulo • Sydney • Tokyo • Toronto

Pergamon Press Offices:

U.S.A.	Pergamon Press, Inc., Maxwell House, Fairview Park, Elmsford, New York 10523, U.S.A.
U.K.	Pergamon Press plc, Headington Hill Hall, Oxford OX3 0BW, England
PEOPLE'S REPUBLIC OF CHINA	Pergamon Press, Xizhimenwai Dajie, Beijing Exhibition Centre, Beijing 100044, People's Republic of China
FEDERAL REPUBLIC OF GERMANY	Pergamon Press GmbH, Hammerweg 6, D-6242 Kronberg, Federal Republic of Germany
BRAZIL	Pergamon Editora Ltda, Rua Eça de Queiros, 346, CEP 04011, Paraiso, São Paulo, Brazil
AUSTRALIA	Pergamon Press Australia Pty Ltd., P.O. Box 544, Potts Point, NSW 2011, Australia
JAPAN	Pergamon Press, 8th Floor, Matsuoka Central Building, 1-7-1 Nishishinjuku, Shinjuku-ku, Tokyo 160, Japan
CANADA	Pergamon Press Canada Ltd., Suite 271, 253 College Street, Toronto, Ontario M5T 1R5, Canada

Copyright © 1991 Pergamon Press, Inc.

Library of Congress Cataloging in Publication Data

Calhoun, Karen S.
    Treatment of rape victims : facilitating psychosocial adjustment / by Karen S. Calhoun, Beverly M. Atkeson.
        p. cm. -- (Psychology practitioner guidebooks)
    Includes bibliographical references.
    Includes indexes.
    ISBN 0-08-031576-3 (hardcover) : -- ISBN 0-08-031575-5 (softcover-pbk.) :
    1. Rape victims--Mental health. 2. Psychotherapy. I. Atkeson, Beverly M., 1949– . II. Title. III. Series.
    [DNLM: 1. Psychotherapy--methods. 2. Rape--psychology. WM 401 C152t]
RC560.R36C35   1991
362.88'3--dc20
DNLM/DLC
for Library of Congress   90-7676
                                             CIP

Printing: 1 2 3 4 5 6 7 8 9   Year: 1 2 3 4 5 6 7 8 9 0

Printed in the United States of America

∞™ The paper used in this publication meets the minimum requirements of American National Standard for Information Sciences—Permanence of Paper for Printed Library Materials, ANSI Z39.48-1984

Contents

Preface

When we began our work with rape victims in the mid-1970s, we were appalled by the lack of information available about the impact of rape and, more so, by the lack of attention in the clinical literature to the needs and problems of victims. Going to the literature for help in treating victims was like confronting a conspiracy of silence. Rape was rarely mentioned, and then usually in passing as though it were a relatively minor event in a person's life. Missing in most of these accounts was the sense of anguish and shattered lives our clients brought to treatment. And the segment of the clinical literature that suggested the problem should be approached by exploring a woman's unconscious desire to be raped was a travesty of treatment.

It was apparent to us, as to a few other groups of researchers, that development of adequate treatment approaches necessitated a thorough understanding of victims' experiences. We therefore undertook an empirical series of studies to investigate patterns of reactions and how victims attempt to cope with them. This work became part of a surge of interest in sexual assault that, over the past decade and a half, resulted in major advances in knowledge about its prevalence and effects. Parallel advances in the understanding of other traumatic events as well as anxiety and affective disorders converged to form the basis for development of new treatment approaches. We have tried in this book to describe some of the methods that have been developed or adapted for use with sexual assault victims and that we have found most helpful. In doing so, we are indebted to those scholars who have had the courage to attempt research and treatment outcome work in this area; in particular, to Dean Kilpatrick, Lois Veronen, and their colleagues at the Medical University of South Carolina; to Patricia Resick; to Judith Becker, Gene Abel, and Linda Skinner; and to Ellen Frank, Barbara Stewart, Sam Turner, and their colleagues.

As such projects tend to do, this one took on a life of its own. In many ways we thought it was too early to attempt a book on treating rape victims, yet we felt a deep responsibility to the millions of victims, past and future, to summarize current thinking in the field. Clinicians all over the country have made us aware of their need for help in understanding and treating victims. We wrote this for them and for the many victims who do not know help is available or who have been disappointed in their efforts to obtain help from mental health professionals. We emphasize, however, that we regard the work presented here as preliminary and far from definitive. There is still much to be learned about the consequences of sexual assault and attempts to cope with them. Thus far, only a handful of controlled treatment studies have been done. We hope to see continued rapid progress in this area and that this book will stimulate interest in developing better ways to help victims.

We wish to acknowledge the assistance of many people in this effort. We thank the National Institute of Mental Health (NIMH) for supporting our research. We thank the many victims who shared their lives with us. We thank Shanna Richman, who coauthored our original grant proposal. Several people helped develop the case studies we have used: Ruth Townsley, Elizabeth Ellis, Ginney Looney, Karen Johnson, and Diane Whitaker. Marilyn Steffe typed and retyped the manuscript with great skill and patience. Thanks are due as well to Ileana Arias, who read portions of the manuscript. Jerry Frank's constant support and tolerance was deeply appreciated. Finally, we wish to thank our families and friends, who bore our neglect and preoccupation, and especially Tom Atkeson, who graciously accepted additional family responsibilities and consistently provided encouragement.

Chapter 1

Sexual Assault in Our Society

Although the last 2 decades have seen a rapid increase in our knowledge concerning the extent and impact of sexual assault on women, much of the existing literature is widely scattered and often not readily accessible. As a result, many clinicians are uninformed when it comes to both general and specific issues in the treatment of rape victims. Yet rape and other forms of sexual abuse, coercion, and harassment affect large numbers of women, many of whom need help in coping with the aftermath or dealing with the long-term psychological impact.

The term *rape* is used here generally to refer to a broad range of types and levels of sexual victimization; not merely to acts that meet narrow legal definitions. The exception is when we report research findings on rape reactions. Most studies use a definition of rape that includes penetration in some form. Rape trauma reactions can be experienced in response to seemingly mild acts of sexual coercion that do not include penetration or physical violence. It is impossible to predict individual reactions. Most studies that have examined average reactions found that it makes little difference whether a sexual assault is attempted or completed, whether the assailant is a stranger, whether a weapon is used, the extent and type of sex acts, and so forth. More important in determining severity of reactions appears to be the level of fear and anticipation of death or injury experienced by the victim during the incident. Her helplessness, enforced passivity, and other forms of humiliation may play an important role as well. Many victims, for example, are forced to verbalize enjoyment of the incident and admiration for the sexual prowess of their attacker.

For purposes of treatment, it is the functioning of the victim that is important, not the type of experience that led to her problems. In this

1

context, any act of sexual domination can be regarded as rape. Treatment goals and methods are largely independent of the incident itself. Precise definitions of types of victimization are, of course, important for legal and research purposes, and the interested reader is referred to Koss and Oros (1982) and Koss and Harvey (1987).

PREVALENCE AND IMPACT

Though estimates of rape prevalence vary, enough methodologically sound surveys have been conducted with consistent enough results that we can say with confidence that between 15% and 25% of women are victims of a completed rape at some point in their lives (Kilpatrick, Veronen et al., 1987; Kilpatrick & Best, 1990; Koss & Harvey, 1987). Other forms of sexual assault, abuse, coercion, and attempted assaults affect greater numbers of women. For example, Koss (1985) found that 75% of female college students had been subjected to some form of unwanted sexual activity. Published crime statistics do not begin to tell the story because the majority of sexual assaults are never reported. A large-scale national probability survey, for instance, found that 84% of sexual assaults had not been reported (Kilpatrick & Best, 1990).

Women and girls of all ages, races, and socioeconomic conditions are vulnerable to rape. Rapes have been reported of infants a few months old and of elderly women in nursing homes. Young women are at greatest risk, however. Child sexual victimization is increasingly recognized as a high-incidence problem, but the incidence of rape among young adolescents has not been as well acknowledged. Ageton (1983) found that 5% to 11% of adolescent girls were assaulted by adolescent boys each year. Age at completed rape was reported by Kilpatrick and Best (1990) for their national probability sample. They found that approximately 25% of rapes occurred before age 10, another 37% between the ages of 11 and 17, and about 25% between 18 and 24. For many women, their first experience with sex is an assault. There is mounting evidence that early victimization puts women at risk not only for psychological dysfunction but for subsequent sexual revictimization.

It is a common misconception that most rapes are attacks by strangers. In reality the opposite is true. Most victims know their attackers (75% in the Kilpatrick & Best, 1990, study). Perhaps the most hidden victims are women raped in the context of marriage and dating relationships. Reliable estimates are difficult to obtain in this area but Russell (1982) found an incidence of 14% among married women and Kilpatrick and Best, (1990) found that 18% of victims had been raped by boyfriends or ex-boyfriends.

Most women who are raped by men they know have difficulty labeling what happened to them as rape, even when it meets the legal definitions.

In spite of recent educational and public media efforts to debunk the myths surrounding rape, it is still commonly believed that most rapists are strangers and that a woman should be able to resist successfully unless the man uses a weapon. Such beliefs confuse and distress acquaintance rape victims, make them reluctant to tell anyone or seek help, and lead victims to look within themselves for a cause of the event. Even victims of rapes by strangers often believe they are responsible somehow for not preventing what happened to them, or that they are permanently defiled by the assault. Thus, guilt, shame, self-blame, and even self-hatred are common among victims. They lose trust in their own judgment as well as trust in others to respect, protect, or empathize with them. Commonly, they attempt to put the incident behind them after initial attempts to work through and integrate it fail. Fear of being overwhelmed by the affect associated with the rape may lead to avoidance, restricted lifestyle, emotional numbness, even amnesia. Intrusive thoughts, nightmares, or flashbacks serve as signals that avoidance and denial are not working, leading to further attempts at suppression. Seeking professional help would mean confronting the incident and exposing one's self to what could amount to reexperiencing the trauma. This helps to explain why so few victims voluntarily seek treatment or delay it for years. When they do seek treatment, they may have denied their affect and cognitively distorted the meaning of their dysfunctions for so long that tracing the connection to the rape is difficult unless therapists are knowledgeable and alert.

THERAPEUTIC CONSIDERATIONS

Therapists who have never worked with rape victims may not realize how challenging they can be. Not only are their problems often multiple and complex, but their lives may have been structured around accommodating the trauma reactions for so long that many layers of issues and emotions must be dealt with. Establishing a working relationship with them can be very difficult because, having been betrayed, they are reluctant to trust anyone and may do a lot of testing in any relationship, especially a therapeutic one. Many are ambivalent, at best, about treatment because it means confronting feelings and issues they may have spent years trying to avoid. This can result in missed sessions, uncooperativeness, and vacillating commitment to therapy (Veronen & Best, 1983). They may be filled with rage and have no available target for it. They can become highly emotional in sessions. Many are hypersensitive to criticism and rejection. Some are suicidal. Some exhibit self-destructive and parasuicidal behavior.

In addition, it is more difficult for a therapist to maintain emotional distance from the trauma than with most other kinds of problems, even other traumas. Discussion of sexual assault can serve as a reminder of one's own vulnerability. Attempts to gain distance can lead to blaming the victim, for example, focusing on something she did that might have precipitated the assault (something you would not do). Koss and Harvey (1987) pointed out that a therapist can feel rejected by the client's refusal to trust or failure to demonstrate commitment to therapy.

Finally, therapists, male and female, must confront their own stereotypes and biases about rape. It is easy to feel empathy for a middle-class victim of a brutal stranger rape, but what about the uneducated woman who accepted a ride and several drinks from a man she met in a bar? Antivictim feelings, biases, and hidden prejudices must all be aired and worked through. If hidden biases come to light after a victim has decided to trust the therapist, it will be experienced as another betrayal and may cause a serious therapeutic setback. One way to prepare for working with victims is through rape awareness sessions or groups offered by many rape crisis centers. Keeping up with the research literature on rape is important as well.

Working with victims can be rewarding in spite of the difficulties. Most are happy to find someone who can help them make sense of their problems and feelings. They can be highly motivated once they have decided to trust the therapist. Sometimes surprisingly rapid gains can be made.

PLAN OF THIS BOOK

The discussion of treatment presented in this book was written with nonrecent, late adolescent or adult victims in mind: nonrecent because the majority of cases clinicians typically see were victimized 2 years or more previously. Because victims often accommodate their lives to the rape aftermath, especially if they were young at the time, they learn to live with their dysfunctions in a way that allows them to ignore them altogether or explain them away. As a result, time elapsed since the rape is a poor predictor of recovery. The "rape core" may be so isolated and covered over that many years pass before something occurs to uncover it. This trigger could be a revictimization, a life change, or a situation demanding that the victim function in ways she cannot.

Many of the issues and treatment approaches covered in this book are relevant and valid for the aftermath of child sexual victimization as well. However, the book was not written specifically with these victims in mind. Rather than diluting the focus of this book to try to cover all the special issues and needs related to child victimization, we think those are best dealt with separately. Clinicians should be aware, however, that many adults they see in treatment may have been victimized as children. Therapists must learn to recognize the cues so this major etiological factor can be integrated into the conceptualization and treatment plan. If it is ignored, treatment often fails.

Post-traumatic stress disorder (PTSD) symptoms are often seen in women victimized as children. A high percentage of women diagnosed with borderline personality disorder have histories of early sexual victimization as well. Specific effects of child victimization often depend on the developmental stage at the time, but some effects are common to all ages. Some of these relate to the self-concept and ability to trust others. Traumatic sexualization often results from offenders' overattention to sexual body parts, rewarding inappropriate sexual behavior and conveying the message that the victim is valuable only insofar as she is sexual. She may come to believe that the only way she can relate to men is sexually, because that is all they value in her. This, combined with the feelings of helplessness that accompany child victimization, puts these girls at risk for later revictimization. Inappropriately seductive behavior and high levels of sexual experience without pleasure should always trigger questions about early sexual victimization. Tragically, these women probably have the greatest risk of unethical sexual exploitation by therapists themselves. This can happen when their behavior is not recognized as part of their pathology or becomes too great a temptation for therapists whose own psychopathology is such that they do not respond in a professional manner to such behavior. This is the ultimate betrayal, when many such women seek therapy as a last resort and are exploited once again.

The following chapters present an overview of the information we think all mental health professionals should know about rape, not only those who knowingly work with victims. Anyone who provides mental health services to women will see rape victims and should take responsibility for gaining adequate knowledge and skills to help them.

Chapter 2 provides an overview of the empirical findings to date on patterns of reactions following rape. Chapter 3 reviews what is known about factors that mediate the patterns of adjustment. Since all victims do not show the same type or severity of reactions, it is clear that some combination of individual, situational, and social factors play a role in individual responses. More research is needed in the area, but a few consistent patterns have begun to emerge. These are discussed with particular regard to demographic variables, prerape functioning, assault-related variables, and postrape variables such as social support.

Crisis intervention is reviewed in chapter 4, which is an introduction to the topic for clinicians who might be called on to provide emergency services to victims. This chapter might be relevant, as well, for those who see victims who have received services from a rape crisis center or who should be considered for referral to such a center. Many therapists find that victims are helped by assistance from rape crisis centers in addition to individual or group therapy. The information they receive about rape and rape reactions and the contact with other victims often helps to normalize their own reactions and provides perspective on them. Rape crisis centers typically work with nonrecent victims in doing crisis counseling.

An overview of assessment is presented in chapter 5, which also emphasizes the importance of developing a meaningful conceptualization of each case that incorporates models of rape reactions. Therapists are encouraged to share this formulation with the woman to help her understand how her problems developed in the context of her own victimization and how proposed treatment plans address goals chosen mutually out of a shared understanding of the problems and their etiology.

The remaining chapters focus on treatment. The final chapter covers special issues for treatment and addresses briefly some important but neglected areas such as adjustment reactions of partners and male victims. The treatment chapters are structured around certain problem areas that are common consequences of rape—anxiety problems, depression, and sexual problems. This is not meant to imply that these problems will be seen unaccompanied by other problems or that they can be treated as isolated problems without attending to the whole picture presented by each case. Many victims have multiple and complex sets of interacting symptom patterns that are challenging to assess and treat. Anxiety and depression frequently coexist. Victims may have sexual problems with no other presenting complaints, but other problems would ordinarily be expected, for example, low self-esteem or lack of assertiveness. When multiple problems are shown, and it is not feasible to address them simultaneously, a decision must be made about their order of importance and the sequence in which they should be addressed. If the wrong choice is made, improvement might be minimal, resulting in discouragement and possibly premature termination. A simple example would be a victim who is both anxious and depressed, but whose depression results from her feelings of helplessness over her inability to control her anxiety. Treatment that fails to address the anxiety problems might not be successful.

The decision about treatment planning should be made conjointly with the victim after full discussion of the alternatives and her reactions to them. An overriding goal in treatment is always to empower the victim to the extent possible, and she should be regarded as a full partner in the process. A distant expert role adopted by a therapist rarely works in any case. Victims respond best to treatment approaches involving development of active mastery skills. These are the approaches we have emphasized.

Some of the chapters contain case examples to illuminate victim reactions or treatment implementation. The case examples are based on real cases or composites of cases, but all names and identifying information have been changed.

Readers may note that we have used the term *victim* throughout, whereas many prefer the term *rape survivor*. We like the positive emphasis implied in discussing survival. It implies active coping and overcoming negative effects of a trauma for which one is not responsible. This helps to put rape victims in the same category as those who suffer other crimes or disasters. On the other hand, it is important to recognize that women who are raped have been victimized through no fault of their own. While this does not mean they are doomed to continue their lives as victims, many do unless they receive help from some source. These are the people clinicians are most likely to see, whether or not their problems are presented as rape induced. This book was written for them.

Chapter 2
Patterns of Reactions

Although individual reactions to sexual assault may vary considerably, discernible patterns have been noted by a number of observers. The major factor determining these patterns is the time elapsed since the assault. Therefore, discussions of victims' reactions and their patterns of adjustment tend to follow a general time sequence. An example is Burgess and Holmstrom's (1974) description of the rape trauma syndrome. They divided reactions into an acute phase, lasting from a few days to several weeks, and a long-term reorganization phase, which may last for years. Other researchers, notably Sutherland and Scherl (1970), have suggested adding a middle stage that has been labeled "outward adjustment" during which the victim appears to return to normal functioning but is actually suppressing the emotional reaction to the assault. Some victims may never progress from this stage to the third stage of reorganization, during which they relive the incident and develop coping mechanisms (sometimes maladaptive) to deal with their reactions.

Ruch and Leon (1983) proposed a model to describe rape reactions that includes two distinct dimensions; effect on the victim and the level of trauma. Adjustment to rape is viewed as a longitudinal process that can be affected at any point by any of a variety of variables including social support, coping mechanisms, preexisting life stresses, and demographic variables such as marital or employment status. The impact of the assault on the victim's life is viewed as a complex interaction between these variables and the type of problem the victim experiences, along with the degree to which the victim is affected by the assault. For example, fear following an assault may be experienced over an extended period of time but the degree of this emotion will vary depending on such events as losing or gaining friends or experiencing other life stresses like the loss of a job or having to testify in court.

SPECIFIC REACTIONS

Fear and Anxiety

A well-documented reaction of sexual assault victims is a persistent pattern of fear and anxiety. Initial reactions during the assault itself set the stage for later problems in this area. Victims almost always report fearing for their lives during a sexual assault. Being under the total domination of another person who is behaving in a threatening and unpredictable way is a terrifying experience whether or not weapons are used or overt threats are made on the victim's life. The victim has no way of knowing what will happen to her and very little opportunity to prevent it. Kilpatrick, Veronen, and Resick (1982) reported that in a large sample of victims, more than 94% said that they felt terrified during the assault and over 90% reported feeling helpless. In addition, extreme physiological manifestations of anxiety are frequently reported. In the same sample, 86% reported trembling or shaking, 80% reported racing heart, 69% muscle tension, and 62% rapid breathing.

Immediately following the assault, victims are usually distraught, although they may show it in different ways. Some are hysterical, crying and expressing fear and distress. Others may become withdrawn and refuse to talk to anyone. During the days and weeks that follow, victims commonly continue to experience nervousness, disruption of concentration, nightmares, emotional reactivity, startle responses, and many other manifestations of anxiety. These reactions tend to decrease over time, but frequently such spontaneous recovery reaches a limit beyond which there is little further improvement in the absence of active intervention. A number of studies have documented the lasting effects of fear and anxiety reactions. Specific phobias may develop, and in some cases even severe agoraphobia.

The enduring nature of fear problems has been well documented in controlled longitudinal studies. For example the victims we followed were significantly more fearful than matched nonvictims at each of six points in time for 1 year following the assault (Calhoun, Atkeson & Resick, 1982). Although a decrease in fear scores occurred during the first 2 months postassault, they leveled off thereafter and no further improvement in average fear scores was seen during the 12-month period (see Figure 2.1). Kilpatrick and Veronen (1983) observed a similar pattern in victims followed up to 3 years after the assault.

Though the level of fear may not change, there do appear to be changes in the patterns of specific feared items. Initially, reported fears seemed to be rape related, such as being alone, weapons, male genitals, and sudden noises. After 6 to 8 months, more classical fears began to emerge (e.g., closed spaces and high places). Fears that reflect feelings of vulnerability

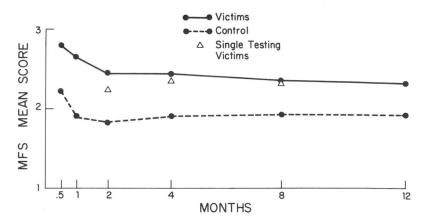

FIGURE 2.1. Modified Fear Survey scores for victim and matched nonvictim comparison groups over a 1-year period following sexual assault. From "A Longitudinal Examination of Fear Reactions in Victims of Rape" by K. S. Calhoun, B. M. Atkeson and P. A. Resick, 1982, *Journal of Counseling Psychology, 29,* pp. 655–661. Copyright 1982 by the American Psychological Association. Reprinted by permission of the publisher.

are also salient (e.g., walking on a dark street or being in a strange place). Testifying in court appears as a commonly feared item, although only a small percentage of rapists are ever brought to trial. It would appear that even the remote possibility of having to relive the experience in public is a frightening prospect.

The fact that fears become somewhat less rape related over time may be a result of generalization to secondary cues or may simply reflect increases in generalized anxiety. However, the decrease in specific rape-related fears may result from victims' avoidance of those things. Victims may report less fear of certain items because they have learned to reduce the risk of exposure to them. Observers, such as Forman (1980), have described a denial phase during which victims minimize problems and appear to function relatively normally. However, this may be at the cost of restricting their lives to avoid cues that would trigger emotional reactions. This avoidance may compound their problems by denying them social interactions of a supportive nature and by making it more difficult to confront fears the longer they are avoided.

Another manifestation of anxiety among rape victims is obsessive-compulsive behavior. This frequently takes the form of checking rituals (e.g., checking locks, checking hiding places in the home for possible attackers). Although these behaviors are understandable consequences of the attack, they can become dysfunctional and resistant to change. Other examples of obsessive-compulsive behavior are washing/cleaning rituals and cognitive rituals. These sometimes bear an obvious relationship to specific circumstances of the attack, but some seem bizarre and unrelated. Too little is understood about the development of these behaviors in relation to sexual assault. It is likely that predisposition plays a role, but research is needed to address the reasons some victims develop these behaviors in preference to other symptoms, what predisposing factors may be involved, and whether full-blown symptoms can be prevented by early intervention.

Depression

Patterns of depressive symptomatology are also well documented in longitudinal studies of rape victims. Depressive symptoms feature prominently in the first few weeks following an assault. Crying spells, sleep and eating disturbances, fatigue, suicidal ideation, and feelings of guilt, worthlessness, and hopelessness are common. Scores on standard depression measures indicate that a high percentage of victims report depression levels above the normal range during the first month. In a study by Frank, Turner, and Duffy (1979), 68% of recent victims fell into this group. Atkeson, Calhoun, Resick, and Ellis (1982) reported that 75% of victims reported mild to severe levels of depressive symptoms during the first month postassault. After 3 or 4 months these levels decreased for most victims to within normal ranges; however, some victims remained depressed. At the end of 1 year Atkeson et al. (1982) found that 26% of victims were still above the normal range of depression, based on their Beck Depression Inventory scores. However, this was not significantly different from the nonvictim group (17%). Figure 2.2 shows the pattern of depression over 1 year.

Depression is a common problem among women, and many may have had problems with depression prior to their assault. However, there are indications that rape contributes uniquely to depressive symptomatology. In either case, intervention may be necessary. The following case is typical.

JoAnn is a 20-year-old woman who works as a secretary for a small business. She was attacked one evening when she stepped outside to the back of the apartment building where she lived alone to take out the trash. A young man she had never seen before was outside and followed her back into the building. When she opened her door he lunged at her and pushed her inside where he raped and sodomized her at knifepoint. After he left she was in a state of shock and just sat, staring, the rest of the night. Once, she tried to call a friend who was not home. The next morning her co-workers took her to the rape crisis center.

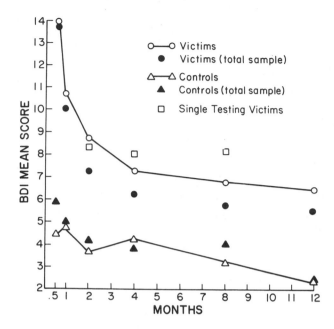

FIGURE 2.2. Beck Depression Inventory scores for rape victims and matched nonraped comparison group over a 1-year period following assault. From "Victims of Rape: Repeated Assessment of Depressive Symptoms" by B. M. Atkeson, K. S. Calhoun, P. A. Resick, and E. M. Ellis, 1982, *Journal of Consulting and Clinical Psychology, 50,* pp. 95–102. Copyright 1982 by the American Psychological Association. Reprinted by permission of the publisher.

JoAnn's boyfriend was supportive and wanted to do anything he could for her. He suggested she move in with him but agreed not to try to have sex until she was ready. During the next few weeks she was unable to work and had to quit her job, after which she stayed at home doing nothing, rarely even bothering to dress. She had nightmares, difficulty sleeping and eating, and lost a lot of weight. Her boyfriend did everything for her, comforted her constantly, and was careful not to push her into doing anything she did not feel like, even eating. His kindness was not helpful, however, making her feel dependent and incapable of doing anything for herself. She began to think about suicide all the time.

The one thing JoAnn was able to do was to visit the rape crisis center where she saw a counselor. She began going daily and staying there a lot during the day, talking to the staff or just sitting. She felt she could not communicate with any of her old friends because she spoke constantly about the assault, which seemed to make them uncomfortable. Her counselor allowed her to talk as much as she wanted about the assault. She went over it again and again, focusing on why it happened, and what she could have done to prevent it or defend herself. Whereas her friends tried to keep her from expressing any self-blame, her counselor helped her put it in perspective.

After 3 or 4 months, JoAnn's depression began to lift and the suicidal thoughts decreased. Her nightmares became infrequent and she began to sleep and eat more regularly, regaining some of the weight she lost. She was still dependent on her boyfriend but took a job and was able to function adequately in spite of her anxiety when strange men came into the office. At first her boyfriend took her home from work every day, but she told him that she needed to learn to do more things for herself and become more independent.

This case shows a typical pattern of depression, with considerable improvement after a few months. JoAnn's depression was more severe than average, however. Her boyfriend may have inadvertently contributed to this by encouraging dependency and being overprotective, thus fostering some feelings of inadequacy.

To illustrate the potential seriousness of the problem, Kilpatrick, Best, Veronen, Amick & Villeponteaux (1985), in a random community survey, found that over 19% of rape victims and 9% of attempted rape victims had attempted suicide. This compared with a 2.2% rate for nonvictims of any crime. In addition, 44% of rape victims reported serious suicidal ideation. Fourteen percent of rape victims reported experiencing "nervous breakdowns" following the assault. George and Winfield-Laird (1986) also found suicidal ideation and deliberate attempts at self-harm to be associated with a history of victimization. Burnam et al. (1988) found that a history of sexual assault increased the risk of major depressive episodes by 2.4 times the rate.

Depressive symptoms may be associated in part with many victims' withdrawal from social interaction and other activities. There is also evidence that victims find many activities in which they participate less reinforcing than prior to the rape. Ellis, Atkeson, and Calhoun (1981a) found that rape victims engaged in pleasant activities to the same extent as nonvictims did but rape victims rated those activities as less pleasurable and less satisfying. This anhedonia is a common feature of depressive disorders.

Also related to depressive symptomatology are the lowered self-esteem and negative changes in self-perception commonly seen in sexual assault victims. One's own feelings of worth may be shattered by being treated like a worthless object by an assailant. This is exacerbated when the victim shares societal beliefs that rape happens only to women who deserve it in some way. The reactions of friends and family, if negative or blaming, can contribute to lowered self-esteem.

Longitudinal studies of victim reactions have found that average self-esteem scores of victims are significantly lower than nonvictims for at least

1 year following the assault (Veronen & Kilpatrick, 1980a). In addition, low self-esteem in victims has been associated with longer recovery time, though the direction of influence could not be determined (Burgess & Holmstrom, 1979a).

Social Adjustment

Sexual assault can disrupt social adjustment in many ways. Social support is believed by many to be an important element in early recovery. Yet rape can disrupt social relationships that might otherwise provide needed support. Social withdrawal and avoidance are common following rape. Many victims move or change jobs, again disrupting social interaction patterns. Going out socially and meeting new people are commonly avoided due to feelings of vulnerability in those situations and/or low self-esteem.

Only a few longitudinal studies have examined specific patterns of social adjustment following sexual assault. Results of Resick, Calhoun, Atkeson & Ellis (1981) illustrate these patterns. The Social Adjustment Schedule Self-Report was used to measure overall social adjustment as well as self-reported functioning in five areas: work or school; social and leisure; economic; marital and family; and extended family. Victims showed severe disruptions in overall social adjustment for the first 2 months after the assault. They gradually improved until, after 4 months, their scores were no longer significantly different from the comparison group of nonvictims. (See Figure 2.3) The pattern for the subscales was similar. Although no significant disruption of marital and family adjustment was shown, extended family relations were disrupted at 1 month postassault and both economic and social/leisure adjustment were disrupted through the 2-month assessment. Disturbance in work adjustment lasted longer, not returning to normal levels until 8 to 12 months postrape. This may reflect several factors including difficulties in concentrating, problems with co-workers or bosses, and time missed from work due to assault-related problems. A few victims changed jobs or lost their jobs. While the economic impact of rape is rarely recognized in the literature, it is a common hardship that contributes to the trauma. Many women hold jobs that pay marginal salaries and benefits and do not allow the flexibility to take time off to deal with personal problems.

An aspect of social adjustment that has been studied in more depth is the relationship with spouse or partner. While reactions vary considerably and seem to depend on the strength of the prerape relationship, for large numbers of victims the trauma is compounded by the loss or serious impairment of partner relationships. Becker, Skinner, Abel, & Treacy

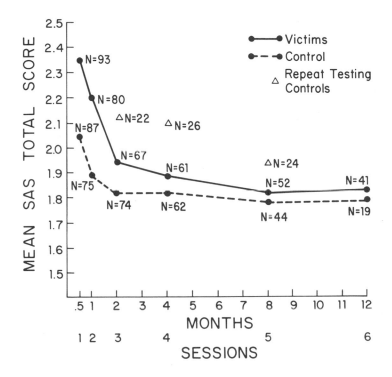

FIGURE 2.3. Social Adjustment Scale scores for victim and matched nonvictim comparison groups over a 1-year period following assault. From "Social Adjustment in Victims of Sexual Assault" by P. A. Resick, K. S. Calhoun, B. M. Atkeson, and E. M. Ellis, 1981, *Journal of Consulting and Clinical Psychology, 49,* pp. 705–712. Copyright 1981 by the American Psychological Association. Reprinted by permission of the publisher.

(1982), for example, reported that 41% of victims had maladjusted partner relationships compared to 21% of nonvictims. Burgess and Holmstrom (1979c) found that 59% of victims in their study had their partner relationships disrupted. These women showed slower recovery from the assault than those whose relationships remained stable.

Sometimes disruption results from a decision not to disclose the assault to the partner and consequent failure of the partner to understand the victim's behavior and emotional state. Such a decision probably reflects the victim's expectation of a negative response to disclosure. When the assault is disclosed, the partner must deal with strong and often mixed emotional reactions while at the same time attempting to be supportive of the victim. The impact of rape on partners must be studied more directly. Partners are a major source of support for victims and their negative reactions (anger, blame, misunderstanding) can be devastating.

Sexual Functioning

It is difficult to generalize about the impact of rape on sexual functioning because individual reactions vary considerably and postassault adjustment in this area, more than in other areas, relies on prerape functioning. A number of studies have documented negative effects on sexual functioning ranging from short-term anxiety to long-term (even lifelong) sexual dysfunctions or avoidance of sex altogether (Ellis, Atkeson, & Calhoun, 1981b). Even when victims show no identifiable sexual dysfunction, there appears to be a general loss of satisfaction associated with sex (Feldman-Summers, Gordon, & Meagher, 1979). Avoidance of sex or reductions in frequency seem to be common early reactions to rape. Whether this becomes a lasting pattern may depend largely on the availability of a sensitive, understanding partner with whom the victim can communicate her feelings and needs, and who lets her set the parameters for resumption of sexual activity. Women who have never been sexually active before the rape have not been studied extensively, but their sexual adjustment may be impaired more than women who have had positive past experiences with sex.

In contrast to victims who avoid sex, victims occasionally react by increasing their frequency of sex and number of partners, usually without concomitant increase in desire or satisfaction. Another reaction observed in some rape victims, as well as adult victims of child sexual abuse, is a normal frequency of sexual intercourse but with strictly limited touching, kissing, or other sex play associated. Thus, they may be orgasmic but still find sex less pleasurable than nonvictims. Sexual touching is avoided because it is not pleasurable and because it triggers negative associations with the assault.

Flashbacks (intense reexperiencing of the trauma to the point of dissociation) similar to those reported by combat veterans are often triggered by sexual contact. A specific act or type of touch, even a word or phrase used by a partner, no matter how loving, may bring on a panic reaction if it mimics the assault in some way. Partners may find this difficult to understand, especially if the victim has difficulty discussing it.

Immediate and long-term disruption of sexual functioning following assault comes from a number of sources. Ellis et al. (1981b) found that the percent of victims who were sexually active increased from 58% 1 month postassault to 77% after 1 year. The number reporting that they enjoyed sex "most of the time" increased from 30% to 45%. The number orgasmic "most of the time" increased only slightly, 29% to 35%. Those reporting flashbacks decreased from 26% to 12%. Feldman-Summers et al. (1979) interviewed victims 2 months to 7 years postassault and found that victim and non-victim groups did not differ in frequency of sexual behaviors or orgasm, but that victims were significantly less satisfied with sex.

These data indicate that sexual problems can be disruptive and persistent. Many women who seek treatment for sexual dysfunctions, although they do not identify themselves as such, are probably long-term sexual assault victims. It may be difficult to provide adequate treatment unless this history is identified and its contribution to current problems recognized.

Somatic Reactions

Reports of physical problems are common in the aftermath of a sexual assault, even when little or no physical injury occurs. Pelvic pain is frequent and may last for days or weeks. Victims are sometimes frustrated by the inability of their physician to identify a specific injury causing the pain. Headaches are commonly experienced by victims, as well as a variety of other aches and pains. These may result from bruising suffered during the attack, but frequently have no obvious source. A thorough physical examination is recommended to rule out hidden physical problems such as venereal disease. In addition, a careful assessment should identify any secondary gains associated with somatic symptoms (e.g., avoidance of sex or social interactions).

Many somatic problems seen in the initial postassault period clear up after a few weeks. Others may become noticeable only after the initial phase, because they have been overshadowed by emotional distress. In some cases, somatic reactions may persist for years. Blanchard and Abel (1976), for example, reported a case of rape-induced tachycardia of many years duration.

Norris and Feldman-Summers (1981) found an increase in several somatic problems when they interviewed victims up to 6 months postassault. Sleep disturbances and eating difficulties were common, as were headaches. The more severe the assault, the more frequently psychosomatic effects were seen.

A recent study illustrates the potential impact of victimization on women's general health. Koss (1988) studied a large sample of women in a worksite-based health maintenance plan that provided full medical coverage. The impact of three types of criminal victimization (rape, physical assault, and burglary) on objective measures of medical services usage was assessed. The design allowed a comparison of usage prior to and following victimization. Of a sample of 2,291 women, 57% had been victims of some type of crime since the age of 14. Of these, 21% were victims of completed rape and 12% of physical assault. According to measures of general health, total symptoms, and mental health, crime victims were less healthy than nonvictims. Women with histories of crime victimization were significantly more likely to visit their physician regardless of when the crime had occurred. Victims of all three crimes studied significantly increased their physician visits between the year of victimization and the following year. Assault and rape victims showed a greater increase than burglary victims. The frequency of visits made by rape victims continued at the same high level even after 2 years. Women who were victims of rape or of both rape and assault had twice as many physician visits as nonvictims. The cost of treating victims was two to three times the cost of treating nonvictims. Level of victimization was the most important predictor of physician visits, outpatient costs, and total medical expenses, contributing over half of the explained variance. In fact, victimization was a more powerful predictor than demographic variables, life stressors other than crime victimization, or even injurious health habits. These results were supported by Phelps, Wallace, and Waigandt (1989), who found sexual assault victims to have more negative perceptions of self-health than nonvictims. They made approximately 35% more visits to their physicians each year. Not only did victims report more present illness symptoms, but they reported more negative health behaviors such as smoking and excessive caffeine or alcohol consumption, which could jeopardize their future health as well.

As illustrated in the following case example, physical symptoms can be vague and their relationship to sexual assault indirect.

> Melinda, 34, was referred to a psychologist by her physician after 6 years of unsuccessful treatment for chronic pelvic pain. No physical basis for the pain had been determined in spite of two hospitalizations for exploratory surgery. At first, Melinda was vague and somewhat defensive. A few sessions of gentle questioning, with an emphasis on building rapport, revealed the following history.
>
> Melinda had dropped out of high school at 17 to marry a 24-year-old auto mechanic. Her primary motive seemed to be a desire to escape from a home in which there was constant conflict and never enough money. She had few friends and responded to Jimmy's attention gratefully. At first their marriage was good. Melinda enjoyed setting up their home and centering her life around Jimmy. But then he began staying out late and drinking heavily on occasion. He became verbally abusive and frequently would end an argument by demanding sex as proof of her love and loyalty. Once, when she refused, he forced her violently. Following that episode she complained of abdominal pain and burning urination for several days but did not seek

medical help. Jimmy was very apologetic, blaming the alcohol for his behavior, and promising it would not happen again. Melinda wanted to believe him, but similar incidents occurred periodically over the course of their marriage. Sex became aversive to Melinda and her lack of interest enraged Jimmy, who believed she had found someone else. He watched her all the time and restricted her contact with other people to the point that she was rarely allowed even to go shopping alone. She considered leaving him, but had no place to go and no way to earn a living for herself and her son.

Melinda's pelvic pain became worse after her pregnancy and Jimmy was often sympathetic, driving her to doctor appointments and refraining from sex when her pain was severe. He became impatient with her constant complaints, however, and his increased demands made her feel worse. It became evident to Melinda's therapist that the pain resulting originally from Jimmy's violence provided the only relief she could find from his abusiveness. The stressful nature of her homelife contributed to and perpetuated the problem. Hospitalizations and doctor visits provided temporary escape from the situation, as well as being her only source of sympathy and support from other people.

Clearly, victimization can have a great impact on physical as well as mental health. The fact that these somatic effects have gone undocumented previously may result from a failure to search systematically for them. Since victims vary in the specific types of symptoms they show, no clear patterns have been obvious. The primary reason, however, that physical symptoms have not been associated with victimization is probably the failure of physicians to discover the history of victimization. Medical schools typically teach little or nothing about rape and its aftermath, and few physicians think to relate physical problems to it.

Other Reactions

Severe debilitating dysfunctions are sometimes seen in sexual assault and sexual abuse victims. For example, approximately half of hospitalized adult psychiatric patients have such histories (Carmen, Rieker, & Mills, 1984). Other disorders in which childhood or adult sexual victimization has been suggested as a significant etiological factor are eating disorders, borderline personality disorder, and multiple personality. Many, if not most, people diagnosed with multiple personality have histories of severe sexual abuse at an early age. In addition, this disorder has been found to be associated with an increased incidence of forcible rape during adolescence and adulthood (Coons & Milstein, 1984). Spiegel (1984) suggested that multiple personality represents a special type of PTSD. The connection between many of these disorders and sexual assault has been studied too little to make definitive causal statements. However, it would appear that the earlier and more severe the trauma, the greater the impact on development and functioning.

Substance abuse has received little recognition in the literature on rape reactions. Yet it is not uncommon and can interfere with positive coping efforts to the extent that the disruption following assault is greatly prolonged. Alcohol appears to be the most common substance abused by victims, with up to 29% of female adult victims reporting excessive use (Frank, Turner, Stewart, Jacob, & West, (1981). Burnam et al. (1988), in a large-scale community sample, found that approximately 16% reported alcohol abuse or dependence and about 18% reported drug abuse or dependence, with onset after sexual assault. This study combined child and adult assault victims as well as male and female victims. Sexually assaulted men were more likely than women to develop later alcohol abuse, but gender did not predict the likelihood of drug abuse (or any other disorder).

The clinical treatment of victims can be more difficult when complicated by drug or alcohol abuse. While substance abuse can be viewed as an attempt at coping, it is clearly self-defeating and usually must be brought under control before treatment can proceed. Referral for specialized treatment of abuse is often appropriate, but should be combined with, or followed by, a focus on treating the rape symptomatology.

Interestingly, the stress of victimization rarely appears to trigger a psychotic break even in predisposed individuals. Burnham et al. (1988), for example, found no difference between sexually assaulted and nonassaulted subjects in lifetime prevalence of schizophrenic disorders. Their results were based on a large, well-controlled study of a community sample. The case of Myra is one of many in which a history of psychosis did not appear to complicate postrape adjustment.

Myra, a heavy-set single woman in her late 20s, had a history of at least three hospitalizations for psychotic reactions, though her memory was vague as to the details. She remembered being given several types of psychotropic medication at various times but, when seen, was not on any medication. She lived at a halfway house and held a series of unskilled jobs, each for brief periods of time. She did not date, had no close friends, and avoided interacting with the other women in the house. Her demeanor was friendly and pleasant, though frequently she appeared somewhat unkempt and laughed or grimaced inappropriately. While walking alone one evening, she was stopped by two men in a car who asked for directions, then pointed a gun and forced her into the car. They drove her to a motel where they forced her to drink alcohol and terrified her with threats. She was raped by both men and forced to perform oral sex. After 3 or 4 hours they fell into a drunken sleep and she was able to flee.

For several days afterwards Myra stayed in her room and avoided everyone, but then forced herself to talk to the other women because she wanted to warn them not to walk alone at night. For 3 weeks, she refused to go out at night, even when accompanied by others, and quit her job. Her mistrust of men was so strong that she refused to talk to a male police officer. However, she showed rapid improvement in mood and functioning. Two months after the assault she took a new part-time job and began dating for the first time in several years. She even reported an interest in having sex. Her mood was positive and she was proud of the confident and assertive way she was able to speak with men, though she still avoided strangers. The way she had cognitively resolved the assault seemed to be important to her functioning. She regarded it as a negative experience but did not dwell on it. When she talked about it, she focused on the strength she had shown in handling the attack and the emotional aftermath. She was pleased that she had remained calm during the attack and made her escape without serious injury.

Four months later Myra continued to do well and showed no signs of psychosis. She had reconciled with her parents, after several years of strained relations, and was making plans to resume her college education.

POST-TRAUMATIC STRESS DISORDER

The American Psychiatric Association's Diagnostic and Statistical Manual (DSM-III-R, 1987) lists rape as an example of a trauma that may induce a PTSD. Although they have unique features, rape victims share many of the same reactions as victims of combat, terrorism, natural disasters, non-sexual crimes, and so forth. These include a wide variety of chronic emotional, behavioral, cognitive, and physiological symptoms such as anxiety, irritability, hostility, emotional lability, social avoidance and distrust, guilt, flashbacks, nightmares, impaired concentration, and extreme physiological reactions in the presence of trauma-related stimuli. Guilt and interpersonal difficulties are also common symptoms.

The DSM-III-R describes PTSD as following "a psychologically distressing event that is outside the range of usual human experience. The stressor producing this syndrome would be markedly distressing to almost anyone, and is usually experienced with intense fear, terror, and helplessness." (p. 247) Duration of the disturbance must be at least 1 month for a diagnosis of PTSD to be made. A delayed onset may occur months, or even years, after the trauma.

Additional diagnostic criteria are:

A. Reexperiencing the trauma in at least one of the following ways:
   1. intrusive and distressing recurrent recollections of the trauma
   2. nightmares
   3. reliving the experience in sudden dissociative episodes (flashbacks)
   4. intense distress in response to events that remind the victim of the trauma
B. Avoidance of stimuli associated with the trauma or numbing of responsiveness, as indicated by at least three of the following:
   1. avoidance of thoughts or feelings associated with the trauma

    2. avoidance of situations that recall memories of the trauma
    3. psychogenic amnesia for all or part of the traumatic event
    4. diminished interest in activities
    5. feeling detached or estranged from others
    6. restricted affect
    7. sense of foreshortened future (and lack of planning)
C. Persistent increased arousal, as seen by at least two of the following:
    1. sleep disturbance
    2. irritability or anger
    3. concentration problems
    4. hypervigilance
    5. exaggerated startle response
    6. physiologic reactivity when exposed to events reminding victim of the trauma

Codisorders are common, such as depression and, in the case of rape, sexual dysfunctions. Thus it may be difficult to make a single diagnosis. A multimethod approach to assessment and treatment is usually indicated as a result. A codiagnosis of schizophrenia would not be common, however, unless the psychotic disorder predated the trauma. Sufferers of PTSD are sometimes misdiagnosed as psychotic, however, if the interviewer fails to uncover the trauma or misses its significance. The flashbacks victims experience may be mistaken for hallucinations if not carefully assessed.

Only preliminary data are available regarding the prevalence of PTSD in rape victims. While most early studies of rape adjustment identified patterns of symptoms indicative of this disorder among some victims, the refinement of diagnostic criteria has evolved more recently. Work on the assessment of PTSD is continuing and should lead to a better understanding of traumatic reactions among rape victims. The incidence rate would appear to be substantial. Preliminary data from a national probability sample of over 1,500 subjects (Kilpatrick, Best, et al., 1989) show that 35% of rape victims had experienced problems that met diagnostic criteria for PTSD. Among victims of attempted rape, the rate was 14%.

Two distinct (though not incompatible) theoretical models have been proposed for PTSD. The first is a learning theory model espoused by several researchers (Becker, Skinner, Abel, Axelrod, & Chichon, 1984; Keane, Zimering, & Caddell, 1985; Kilpatrick, Veronen & Best, 1985;). Incorporating Mowrer's (1960) two-factor theory, it postulates that victims can become conditioned to a wide variety of stimuli during a traumatic event, even to cognitions. Later exposure to these stimuli evokes a conditioned emotional response. Higher order conditioning can produce the same response to new cues not present at the assault, by pairing with the original conditioned stimuli. Through stimulus generalization, additional stimuli come into play due to similarity with the conditioned stimuli. The victim tries to avoid these aversive situations, thoughts, and feelings. Avoidance is negatively reinforcing but becomes increasingly difficult as more and more stimuli become associated with the memory. Avoidance and other factors preclude complete exposure, so the traumatic response is never extinguished. By the time victims seek treatment, this process may be so far along that it necessitates a complex treatment program that ensures all elements of the memory are fully exposed, including the relevant affective or cognitive state.

A further refinement of the learning theory model has been proposed by Foa, Steketee, and Olasov-Rothblum (1989). It incorporates the importance of cognitive interpretation of events (meaning), based on such findings as that perceived threat predicts PTSD better than objective threat. It is based, in part, on Lang's (1979) bio-informational theory of affect in which the meaning properties of images are as important as the stimulus and response properties. Emotional processing of information comprising the emotional image (including meaning) is the essential approach to anxiety reduction. Emotional processing, defined as the modification of memory structures that underlie emotions, requires exposure to corrective information (Foa & Kozak, 1986). Within the traumatic experience, unpredictability, along with uncontrollability, is seen as contributing to a higher likelihood of PTSD. While all rapes are perceived by victims as uncontrollable, they vary in predictability.

A biological model of PTSD has been proposed by Van der Kolk, Greenberg, Boyd, and Krystal (1985). It postulates that the biochemical effects of inescapable aversive stimulation in animals can be used as a model for traumatic stress effects in humans. Specifically, decreases in central levels of norepinephrine following acute stress could account for the deficit symptoms (such as anhedonia, social withdrawal, restricted affect), while symptoms such as exaggerated startle responses and angry outbursts might be associated with noradrenergic overreactivity to trauma-relevant stimuli. Further, endogenous opioids are thought to be released during a trauma and their subsequent depletion may be experienced as aversive, setting up a cycle of behavior that reexposes the victim to stress repeatedly in an attempt to regain the analgesic effects of the endogeneous opioids. It should be emphasized that this model has not been well tested but it fits the pattern shown by many combat-related PTSD sufferers as well as many cases of borderline personality disorder.

Evidence is mounting in support of such a biological model (cf. Krystal et al., 1989). For example, Kosten, Mason, Giller, Ostroff, and Harkness (1987) found that urine epinephrine and norepinephrine levels of PTSD inpatients were significantly higher than inpatients diagnosed with schizo-phrenia or affective disorders. A number of neurotransmitter systems ap-pear to be involved in PTSD, even though research is complicated by the high rates of comorbidity with other neurobiologically influenced dis-orders such as depression, panic disorder, and alcoholism. A detailed re-view of the evidence is beyond our scope here, but it would appear that high levels of experienced trauma may result in long-term dysregulation of the noradrenergic and other systems, resulting in development of learned alarm responses and disturbances in memory regulation. It has been suggested that PTSD could involve fundamental neuronal changes including alterations in structure and gene expression (Krystal et al., 1989). The withdrawal, emotional numbing, and dissociation commonly ob-served in PTSD sufferers could be viewed as attempts to reduce over-whelming stimulation to a damaged central nervous system. Similarly, the irritability, hypervigilance, and angry outbursts might be interpreted as symptoms of such impaired functioning.

Rape victims seem more likely than combat veterans to withdraw. The angry, sometimes violent, outbursts seen in combat-related PTSD sufferers are rare in rape victims, although 57% in one study reported vengeful fantasies (Resick, 1987). In fact, surprise at the apparent lack of anger many victims show toward their assailant is often expressed by others. Victims frequently make excuses for the assailant, (e.g., "He must be sick to do such a thing. He needs help."). While this may represent an attempt to get some control over the experience by making sense of it, it also points up the poorly understood but potentially important role of anger in the ad-justment of victims.

A number of explanations are possible for the differences between rape-related and combat-related PTSD in the way anger is handled. First, it is not clear that explosive expressions of anger are actually rare in rape victims, if we consider only those diagnosable as PTSD sufferers. Few of the major studies of rape victims published to date have attempted to make such diagnoses because too little was known about the criteria until re-cently. Secondly, gender differences must be taken into account. Male rape victims have been studied so little that hardly anything is known about their patterns of adjustment. The socialization of women is counter to anger expression. They have not been socialized, as have many men, to behave aggressively in reaction to heightened emotional states. And they have not had combat training. For many men, angry and aggressive behav-ior may be instrumental (Wolfe, Keane, Lyons, & Gerardi, 1987). It has been positively reinforced because frequently it results in immediate, though short-term, desired changes in the environment (i.e., in other peo-ple's behavior). For women, anger expression is more often associated with punishment. Anger can also be used to counter anxiety, a strategy more available as well as more acceptable to many men.

Finally, the extremes of anger expression seen in the two groups— female rape victims' frequent inability to express or even experience anger and some combat veteran PTSD sufferers' frequent explosive outbursts— may be viewed as two sides of the same coin, the reduced capacity for modulation and fear of losing control described in DSM-III-R. Preoccupation with losing control sometimes leads to social withdrawal, contributing to further problems (e.g., depression). The emotional numbing seen in so many victims of all types of trauma also serves as an aid in retaining emotional and behavioral control. This numbing and anhedonia can be intractable and frequently remains after other aspects of the syndrome have been successfully treated (Keane, 1988).

It appears probable that biological predisposition interacts with trauma experience in the development of PTSD. Family studies, though preliminary, support the familial aggregation of psychopathology in veterans with PTSD. Davidson, Swartz, Storck, Krishnan, & Hammett, (1985) found rates of depression and anxiety in families of veterans with PTSD similar to rates for matched samples of nonveterans with generalized anxiety disorder and higher rates of anxiety disorder than in nonveterans with major depression. Foy, Resnick, Sipprelle, and Carroll (1987) found higher rates of PTSD diagnosis in veterans with family psychopathology than in those without it (48% and 27%/30% and 11% respectively in two different samples). However, these figures were for veterans with low exposure to combat. For veterans with high combat exposure (including being wounded), a high rate of PTSD (70%) was found regardless of the rate of family psychopathology. Other studies support the primacy of trauma intensity and duration in the etiology of PTSD (e.g., Foy, Sipprelle, Rueger, & Carroll, 1984; Frye & Stockton, 1982), and it has been estimated that 40% of the variance is predicted by degree of combat exposure (Foy et al., 1984). This research needs to be extended to victims of other types of trauma.

Other factors that might predispose trauma victims to PTSD have received less attention in the literature. However, certain types of previous experiences may play an important role. For example, previous victimization has been consistently correlated with greater disruption in functioning of rape victims (see chapter 3). Race and family stability played a role in one study of war veterans (Egendorf, Kadershin, Laufer, Rothbart & Sloan, 1981).

Barlow (1988) proposed a model for the etiology of PTSD that takes into account the predisposing biological vulnerability and subsequent chain of events, including possible moderating effects of social support

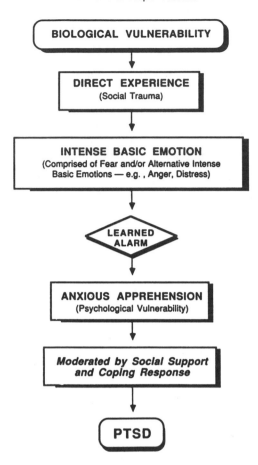

FIGURE 2.4. A model of the etiology of PTSD. From *Anxiety and Its Disorders* (p. 507) by D. H. Barlow, 1988, New York: Guilford. Copyright 1988 by Guilford Press. Reprinted by permission.

and coping skills (see Figure 2.4). With the addition of early experiences (e.g., child abuse, family environment) as predisposing factors that might increase vulnerability, it would account for most of the empirical evidence to date. Rapid advances are being made in the understanding of PTSD and with them we can expect the refinement of theoretical models.

Chapter 3
Mediating Factors in Victim Reactions

Although the major impetus of initial research efforts with sexual assault victims has been to document a fairly uniform pattern of traumatic response to rape, individual variability in the psychological sequelae continue to be noted as well. That is, while most victims exhibit significant disruption in their lives and experience psychological dysfunction along a number of dimensions immediately following rape and for at least the first few months thereafter, significant differences in the severity and duration of the distress are also apparent. Variability in the specific symptomatology and degree of impairment are also observed in nonrecent victims.

Intuitively, this observation is not surprising. Victims vary widely in terms of their demographic characteristics, the availability and quality of their social support systems, and their experiences and functioning prior to the assault. Characteristics of the assault can also be different. As a result, several studies have attempted to identify variables which might affect the victim's risk for severe and/or prolonged reaction to rape. To date the results have been mixed with few clear patterns emerging. Because the purpose of this book is not to provide a methodological critique of current research efforts, suffice it to say that these studies have varied in terms of methodological sophistication, sample selection, statistical procedures, dependent and criterion measures, and time elapsed since the assault—some or all of which may have contributed to the conflicting results. However, for the clinician working with victims of sexual assault it is important to be aware of the varying factors which might affect an individual's immediate and long-term response to rape and to keep these factors in mind during assessment, treatment planning, and treatment implementation and evaluation.

DEMOGRAPHIC VARIABLES

Research on victim demographic variables, such as age, race, and socio-economic status, and victim reactions to assault have yielded mixed findings. Most studies find that the age of the victim at the time of the assault either has no effect on subsequent reactions (Cohen & Roth, 1987; Frank & Stewart, 1983; Kilpatrick, Veronen, & Best, 1985; Ruch & Leon, 1983) or that older women have more difficult adjustments following assault (Atkeson, Calhoun, Resick, & Ellis, 1982; Burgess & Holmstrom, 1974; Frank & Stewart, 1984; Ruch & Chandler, 1983; Sales, Baum, & Shore, 1984). The label *older* must be interpreted cautiously, however. For example, in Atkeson et al.'s (1982) study, 75% of the victims were below the age of 30, although some participants were middle aged and older. Thus, failure of some studies to find a relationship may result from a restricted age range. However, it may also be the case that older victims are more likely to endorse traditional beliefs concerning rape, are more likely to restrict their activities following assault, have less social support, or are less resilient.

Fewer studies have examined the effect of victim race but the results have been more consistent. Comparisons between white and black victims show no differences in severity of reactions (Frank & Stewart, 1983; Kilpatrick, Veronen, & Best; 1985) or recovery rate (Morelli, 1981). However, Ruch and Chandler (1983) found that Asian victims suffered greater trauma than Caucasian victims. Ethical and/or cultural beliefs and values may interact with other assault variables such as social support and victim attributions to exacerbate or delay victim recovery.

Most studies which have examined socioeconomic level and victim outcome report that poor women exhibit more long-term disturbance on specific measures of fear, depression, and social adjustment (Atkeson et al., 1982; Cohen & Roth, 1987) and more global measures of distress (Burgess & Holmstrom, 1978). Because of their economic situation, poor women tend to live in high crime areas with the continued risk of victimization. This stress combined with other stresses associated with poverty may retard recovery or may separately contribute to the occurrence of symptomatology.

Victim employment may exacerbate adjustment (McCahill, Meyer, & Fischman, 1979) especially in the first few months following assault when the victim's acute distress impairs her ability to function adequately on the job. However, Ruch and Leon (1986) found that employment facilitated recovery for nonrecent victims. Once the initial distress dissipates to more manageable levels, a job may provide structure, regular social contact, and a moderate level of activity—all of which may be of benefit to the victim's recovery. Many of the victims in our own study either quit or were fired from their jobs during the first few months following their assault and only later attempted to reenter the job market. Similarly, student victims frequently dropped out of school within a few weeks following the assault.

Burgess and Holmstrom (1979c) reported that victims with stable partners recovered more quickly following assault. Other researchers have found no relationship between marital status and victim reaction (Frank & Stewart, 1983; Kilpatrick, Veronen, & Best, 1985); whereas others have reported that married victims have greater postrape adjustment problems (McCahill et al., 1979; Ruch & Chandler, 1983). Concerning this lack of consistency, Steketee and Foa (1987) pointed out that "being married does not necessarily imply a stable or positive relationship" (p. 75). In some cases, being married may make it more difficult to avoid sexual relations for a period of time following the assault and/or attempts to avoid intimacy may lead to increasing conflict within the relationship.

ASSAULT CHARACTERISTICS

Earlier studies which examined the relationship between certain assault characteristics and subsequent victim reactions reported several interesting and intuitively reasonable outcomes. Burgess and Holmstrom (cited in Bennetts, 1978) reported that the length of recovery following assault was affected by specific factors within the assault situation. Women attacked without warning (a "blitz" rape) had a more difficult recovery than women whose assailant gained their trust prior to the assault (a "con" rape). The location of the assault also prolonged recovery; women who were attacked while sleeping in their own bedrooms reported greater disturbance 5 years following the assault. Seeming to contradict these findings, Burgess and Holmstrom (1979) subsequently reported that victims raped by persons known to them experienced greater disturbance because they had the additional task of reevaluating their judgment concerning interpersonal trust. Victims of multiple assailants also required a longer recovery time because resolution involved dealing with each assault individually.

Subsequent studies, using standardized assessment instruments to measure victim reactions, have for the most part failed to support Burgess and Holmstrom's findings. The type of assault (con vs. blitz) has not been found to predict either short- or long-term victim reactions on measures of fear, anxiety, depression, or social adjustment (Frank, Turner, & Stewart, 1980; Santiago, McCall-Perez, Gorcey, & Beigel, 1985). Similarly, the location of the assault does not appear to affect levels of victim fear, anxiety, depression, or social adjustment (Frank et al., 1980; Kilpatrick, Veronen, & Best, 1985). The impact of multiple assailants is less clear. Girelli, Resick, Marhoefer-Dvorak, and Hutter (1986) found that multiple assailants did not increase victim fear and anxiety. Using a more global measure of distress, Kilpatrick, Veronen, and Best (1985) also found that the presence of multiple assailants did not contribute to victim symptomatology; however, Sales et al. (1984) found that victims of multiple assailants reported significantly more fear, anxiety, and depression than victims of single assailants both immediately following the assault and at various time periods postassault.

In another early study, Bart (1975) found that the victim's relationship with the assailant prior to the assault seemed to affect the type of difficulties which developed following the assault. Thirty-two percent of the women raped by strangers reported that they developed postrape sexual problems. In contrast, 46% of the women raped by dates and 73% of the women raped by lovers or husbands reported that they became sexually dysfunctional. The Queen's Bench Foundation (1976) also reported differential reactions to assault as a function of the victim's relationship with the assailant. However, they found that women raped by strangers showed greater disturbance in their sexual functioning, in addition to problems with self-image and feelings about personal safety. Women who were assaulted in the assailant's home (implying some prior relationship with the assailant) showed more impairment in their social functioning than women raped by strangers. The threat and/or use of physical force also resulted in more overall trauma and especially affected a woman's self-image, social relations, and sexual functioning.

Again subsequent studies, using standardized assessment instruments to measure victim reactions, have generally failed to find a relationship between the stranger–nonstranger dichotomy and victim levels of fear, anxiety, depression, and social adjustment (Frank et al., 1980; Girelli et al., 1986) or global indices of mental health (Kilpatrick, Best, Ruff, Veronen, & Ruff, 1985). Ellis, Atkeson, and Calhoun (1981a) in their examination of long-term reactions to sexual assault did find that women raped by strangers had more severe reactions, being even more depressed, fatigued, and fearful, and obtaining less satisfaction from activities than victims of nonstranger assaults. However, in that study, degree of familiarity with the assailant had much to do with factors within the assault situation. Rapes by strangers involved significantly more violence and trauma as measured by weapons, threats, injury, length of attack, and number of sex acts committed.

Unfortunately, studies examining the impact of both specific and global indices of violence within the assault have not yielded consistent results either. Several studies have failed to find a relationship between victim reactions and single assault characteristics, such as verbal threats, presence of weapons, physical injury, number and type of sex acts committed, and length of the assault, and/or summary measures of the degree of assault violence (Atkeson et al., 1982; Frank et al., 1980; Girelli et al., 1986; Kilpatrick, Veronen, & Best, 1985; Santiago et al., 1985). Other studies have found that the more violent the assault, the more severe the victim reaction (Cohen & Roth, 1987; McCahill et al., 1979; Norris & Feldman-Summers, 1981; Orlando & Koss, 1983; Sales et al., 1984). Interestingly, McCahill et al. (1979) reported a curvilinear relationship between rape violence and postrape adjustment. Both victims of brutal rape and victims whose assaults fell at the lower end of the continuum with respect to violence were found to have more adjustment difficulties. Concerning the latter, McCahill et al. (1979) noted, "Here the victim is more likely to be blamed for failure to resist the assault or even for trying to cover up consensual sexual activity" (p. 71). Frank and Stewart (1983) also found that victims who experienced "minimal brutality" showed poorer adjustment in the immediate family.

Several factors may be important in understanding the lack of consistency. Victims of more brutal rapes, especially those requiring hospitalization, may not participate in studies assessing short-term reactions to sexual assault. However, studies of nonrecent rape victims usually rely on advertisement campaigns to obtain participants and may be biased in other equally important ways. Random samples of victims of nonrecent sexual assault do find a relationship between physical injury and global mental health problems and the diagnosis of PTSD (Kilpatrick, Best, Ruff et al., 1985). Perhaps victims of more violent rapes show initial patterns of distress similar to those of less violent rape victims but experience more prolonged and serious reactions in the years following the assault.

Objective indices of violence and brutality may be less important than the victim's subjective experience. Accordingly, Sales et al. (1984) suggested, "It is possible that the actual violence of an attack is less crucial to victim reaction than the felt threat" (p. 125). The few studies that have examined the relationship between the victim's subjective distress during the assault and subsequent functioning found that subjective distress and cognitive appraisal of danger predicted victim fear and anxiety, general mental health problems, and diagnosis of PTSD better than severity of the assault (Girelli et al., 1986; Kilpatrick, Veronen et al., 1987).

HISTORICAL VARIABLES

Prior Psychological Functioning

A history of physical, psychiatric, or social difficulties (e.g., alcohol and drug abuse, psychiatric hospitalization or treatment) has consistently been shown to compound a victim's initial reaction and inhibit her general long-term recovery (Burgess & Holmstrom, 1974, 1978). Preexisting mental health or substance abuse problems are influential variables affecting level of trauma during the early (up to 2 weeks) postassault period (Ruch & Leon, 1983). In the study by Frank et al. (1981), over one third of the victims reported some type of mental health contact prior to the assault. However, only victims with a history of psychotropic medication, suicidal ideation, or suicidal attempts showed significantly more dysfunction on all their standardized measures of depression, anxiety, and social adjustment during the first month postassault. Ruch and Chandler (1983) also reported that 30% of the victims in their study had preexisting emotional or sub-stance abuse problems, including generalized anxiety, depression, suicidal ideation, or alcoholism, and that such factors reduced the victim's ability to deal with the emotional crisis produced by the assault and significantly elevated the initial reaction to the assault. Using the Diagnostic Interview Schedule (Robins, Helzer, Croughan, & Ratcliff, 1981) Frank and Anderson (1987) determined whether victims met DSM-III (APA, 1980) criteria for either a past or current psychiatric disorder. Those victims with a prior diagnosis were significantly more likely than victims without such a his-tory to meet diagnostic criteria for a current disorder during the first month following assault.

Prior functioning appears to have a similar impact on long-term recov-ery. Atkeson et al. (1982) found that women with psychological problems prior to the assault, and in particular problems with anxiety, obsessive-compulsive behaviors, and depression, were more likely to experience a slower recovery with respect to depressive symptoms. Also, problems with sexual relationships and poor physical health prior to the rape adversely affected the duration and severity of depressive symptoms. Miller, Wil-liams, and Bernstein (1982) also found that previous psychiatric treatment and/or a history of alcohol and drug abuse was related to more chronic problems in victims' sexual functioning and marital relations following assault. Finally, preexisting psychopathology is listed as a predisposing factor in the development of PTSD (DSM-III-R, APA, 1987).

Prior Life Stress

Effects of life stress prior to the assault are complex, requiring the specification of the severity, duration, and length of time elapsed since the stressor. Burgess and Holmstrom (1978) reported that a history of chronic stress (e.g., low income, social isolation) inhibited victims' recovery over a 4- to 6-year period following assault. Of course, such chronic factors could be expected to continue to exist during the postassault period and could also directly affect recovery. Following assault a victim with chronic life stressors has to continue to cope with the preexisting stressors and has the additional burden of dealing with her assault. A victim with chronic life stress also has fewer resources (e.g., the financial means to move to a safer neighborhood, the emotional support of friends) to help her cope with the assault crisis.

In contrast, some preassault stressors were found to facilitate recovery. Victims who had lost a family member as a result of death, separation, or divorce more than 2 years prior to the assault recovered more quickly than victims who had not experienced such a loss. Burgess and Holmstrom (1978) speculated that victims undergoing a major crisis prior to the assault acquired coping skills which facilitated their recovery when assaulted. Later research has suggested that victims must have sufficient time to recover from a major life stress or such a factor will exacerbate the assault reaction. Kilpatrick, Veronen, and Best (1985) found that victims who had lost a family member in the year prior to the assault exhibited more distress following assault than victims who had not experienced such a loss. Evidently, major losses prior to the assault can facilitate or impair recovery depending on the time elapsed since the loss and adjustment to it. Supposedly, sufficient time must have passed for the victim to resolve the loss and acquire additional coping skills if such a loss is to facilitate rape recovery.

Ruch and her colleagues (Ruch & Chandler, 1983; Ruch, Chandler, & Harter, 1980; Ruch & Leon, 1983) have also examined the impact of life change events during the year prior to the assault on rape adjustment. The life change events varied from minor (e.g., moving) to major (e.g., death of a spouse) and included both positive (e.g., marriage, birth of a child) and negative (e.g., divorce, separation) events. They found a curvilinear relationship between prior life change and rape impact. Women who had experienced major life changes exhibited the most trauma, women with no changes experienced intermediate levels of trauma, and women with mild changes showed the least trauma. The qualitative nature of the life change event (i.e., whether it was positive or negative) did not significantly affect the level of rape trauma. The critical factor appeared to be the amount of life change. Ruch and Chandler (1983) hypothesized that the recent experience of handling relatively manageable life change enhances a person's self-confidence and coping skills in dealing with the victimization. In contrast, victims with major life changes or with no life changes are more vulnerable and less able to cope with the assault.

A number of studies have examined the effect of a specific life event, prior sexual victimization, on adjustment to rape. Unfortunately the results have not been consistent. Ruch and Chandler (1983) found that victims with a history of prior sexual assault were significantly less traumatized immediately following the current assault than victims experiencing their first assault. They hypothesized that "perhaps victims who have survived other rapes . . . have developed coping skills to deal with the severe stress evoked by a sexual assault" (p. 182).

However, a subsequent study by Ruch and Leon (1983) illustrated the importance of assessing victims over time. They found that women who had been victimized before had a relatively low level of trauma initially, but became more severely traumatized within 2 weeks when compared to victims experiencing their first assault. These findings imply that there may be significant delayed effects of prior sexual assault on victim recovery, at least for the short term. Victims with a prior assault history may have intensified feelings of vulnerability, lack of control, and self-blame. Prior sexual assault victims may also be more likely to have continuing psychological problems from the first assault, and these preexisting problems may compound the victim's recovery.

Using standardized assessment instruments to evaluate victim adjustment during the first month following rape, Frank et al. (1980) found that women who had been sexually assaulted prior to the current assault had poorer social adjustment, especially with their immediate families, but were no more symptomatic on depression and anxiety measures than women without a prior assault. Also, women who had a history of sexual victimization were at significantly higher risk for developing a major depressive disorder during the first month postassault (Frank & Stewart, 1984). However, in a subsequent study examining the prevalence of other psychiatric diagnoses in addition to major depressive disorder, Frank and Anderson (1987) found that victims who had experienced a prior victimization were not at greater risk for a psychiatric disorder than victims with no prior assault history. Explanations of the inconsistencies in these findings by the same research group are difficult to make.

The effect of prior sexual assault on long-term reactions has also been examined. Multiple-incident victims have been found to have higher overall symptomatology, somatization, depression, anxiety, hostility, paranoid ideation, and psychoticism (Cohen & Roth, 1987; Santiago et al., 1985). McCahill et al. (1979) reported that multiple-incident victims had more intense nightmares and greater fears of being home but were not different in other ways from single-incident victims at 1 year postassault.

Several studies have examined the effects of other types of victimization on subsequent adjustment to rape. Burgess and Holmstrom (1978, 1979b) included a history of attempted or completed sexual assault, assault, mugging, or verbal or physical sexual harassment under their assessment of prior victimization and found that victims with a history of prior victimization showed impaired recovery 4 to 6 years after the assault. Glenn and Resick (1986) examined the effects of prior victimization within the family (i.e., a history of spouse violence, child abuse, incest, or observed parental violence) on adjustment to subsequent rape. As predicted, prior experience with family violence was shown to increase the severity of reaction and hinder recovery in several areas of the victim's life.

SOCIAL SUPPORT

The stress research literature has given increasing attention to the variable social support—the hypothesis being that support buffers the effects of stress and thus moderates the impact of stressful life events on subsequent functioning. Not surprisingly then, several researchers in the area of sexual assault have examined the mediating effects of social support on victim recovery.

As with many other moderating variables, the findings have been somewhat inconsistent and may be due, in part, to complex interactions between social support and other mediating factors. Obviously, postassault support is influenced by the quality and quantity of preassault relationships. Furthermore, victims with a poor social network prior to the assault may differ in their overall preassault functioning. Variables within the assault may also influence the reactions of the victim's support system after the assault. Several studies have found that the more brutal the assault the better the victim's postassault relationship with family members (Frank & Stewart, 1983; Sales et al., 1984). Initial reactions of the victim's social network may also compound or exacerbate the victim's postassault adjustment. Not surprisingly, the concept of secondary trauma has been introduced in which the victim of sexual assault subsequently is held responsible for the event (Foy et al., 1987; Janoff-Bulman, 1982; Kilpatrick, Veronen, & Resick, 1982). Finally, the level of the victim's distress following sexual assault interacts with her ability to develop and utilize social support to facilitate recovery. Victims whose initial distress is more severe may be less able to mobilize a supportive network to moderate their distress.

Simple indices of social support have been found to be positively related to overall adjustment. For example, Cohen and Roth (1987) reported that taking longer to confide in another person following assault was significantly associated with worse overall adjustment. When global indices are used, social support has been found to be positively related to both immediate and long-term recovery. Burgess and Holmstrom (1978) reported that 45% of the victims with social support felt recovered within months after their assaults; whereas none of the victims without social support felt recovered within the same time frame. Similarly, 4 to 6 years following the assault, 80% of the victims with social support felt recovered; whereas only 47% of the victims without social support did. The quality of the social support may also be important. Frank (1984) found that victims who perceive one or more important members of their social network as unsupportive are more symptomatic overall during the first month postassault than victims with all neutral and/or supportive network members.

The results of several studies have suggested the importance of family relationships in mediating victim adjustment. Resick (1981) found that a victim's reported relationship with her parents was significantly related to her postassault psychological functioning on a number of measures. Sales et al. (1984) found that although neither the initial reactions of significant others in the victim's social network nor the quality of the victim's significant relationship with a man was related to her immediate recovery, by 6 months postassault, victims reporting greater closeness to family members had fewer symptoms. Family relationships were also the most potent predictor of long-term severity.

Other studies have suggested that initial support may have delayed effects on victim adjustment. Atkeson et al. (1982) found that the victim's report of social support immediately following the assault predicted depressive symptoms at 4 and 8 months postassault. Such a delayed effect suggests that the immediate response of the victim's social network may shape later beliefs and cognitions as the victim assimilates the stressful event.

COPING STRATEGIES

Coping strategies include both cognitions and behaviors that a victim may use to manage, reduce, or recover from the emotional distress and disruption in daily functioning resulting from sexual assault. Within this framework, coping strategies may be characterized as either adaptive or maladaptive and their use may either facilitate or impede a victim's recovery.

Although research on coping in response to sexual assault is limited to a handful of studies, the results have successfully delineated a number of strategies which are significantly related to victim recovery. Based on victims' self-reported length of time "to feel recovered" and their qualitative descriptions of coping, Burgess and Holmstrom (1979a) found that victims who used one or more conscious cognitive strategies to master the anxiety generated by the rape felt recovered more quickly. These cognitive strategies included explanation (developing a reason for the rape), minimization (viewing what happened to them as better than other possible traumatic experiences), suppression (controlling and/or avoiding thoughts about the rape), and dramatization (repeatedly talking about the rape and one's feelings). Victims who responded to the rape by increasing their activity level (e.g., moving, visiting friends or relatives, traveling) also showed a quicker recovery. Maladaptive responses were those associated with longer self-reported recovery and included a marked decrease in activity level (e.g., withdrawing from social contacts, staying home) and self-destructive behaviors (e.g., suicide attempts, substance abuse).

The relationship between different coping strategies and objective indices of fear, anxiety, depression, and overall adjustment has also been examined (Burt & Katz, 1987; Frazier, 1989; Meyer & Taylor, 1986). Like Burgess and Holmstrom (1979a), certain coping approaches were found to be associated with relatively better adjustment, whereas others were not. Keeping busy, thinking positively, and suppression were associated with decreases in depression. Practicing specific stress reduction techniques was associated with decreases in fear and depression. Staying home and withdrawing from others was associated with increased levels of depression and anxiety. And nervous/anxious behaviors and self-destructive behaviors correlated negatively with overall adjustment. When directly asked what they had done since the assault that had been helpful, victims most often mentioned obtaining support from family and friends, expressing feelings or talking about the rape, making life changes, using precautionary behaviors, and entering counseling (Frazier, 1989; Meyer & Taylor, 1986).

Interestingly, several studies have found a positive relationship between coping strategies of any type and negative symptomatology (Burt & Katz, 1987; Cohen & Roth, 1987; Wirtz & Harrell, 1987b). Both Burt and Katz (1987) and Wirtz and Harrell (1987b) suggested that more coping strategies are used and endorsed when negative symptomatology is high; as symptoms decrease, fewer coping strategies are needed and consequently fewer are used. In support of this interpretation, Burt and Katz also found negative correlations between coping and self-ratings of recovery. Victims reported that they were less recovered when they were still actively coping with the rape.

One unresolved issue in the area of coping concerns the victim's causal attributions for the assault and their effect on victim recovery. Earlier it was noted that victims who were able to develop an explanation for the assault recovered more quickly (Burgess & Holmstrom, 1979a). Even explanations in which the victim focused on herself resulted in shorter recovery times. Burgess and Holmstrom (1979a) argued that the explanations facilitated recovery because they served to decrease anxiety. Furthermore, although victims blamed themselves for their decisions or behavior, they did not feel guilty about their actions.

Concerning causal attributions, Janoff-Bulman (1979) proposed that a distinction should be made between behavioral and characterological self-blame. Within her theoretical framework, behavioral self-blame is an adaptive response in which the victim assigns responsibility for the rape to her own modifiable behaviors (e.g., "I should have locked my car.") and may help the victim reestablish a sense of control over her life. In contrast, characterological self-blame is a maladaptive response and involves negative attributions to one's own character (e.g., "I'm a weak person.").

While intuitively appealing, the aforementioned distinction between behavioral and characterological self-blame and the differential effect of such attributions on victim recovery has not received empirical support. Both types of self-blame have been found to correlate positively with fear, depression, and sexual satisfaction (Meyer & Taylor, 1986). That is, the more a victim attributed blame to herself (either behavioral or characterological) the more severe her postrape symptomatology. Although they failed to differentiate between the two types of self-blame, Katz and Burt (1988) also found that higher degrees of self-blame were associated with greater distress following assault and that over time, as part of the recovery process, victims shifted the blame for the assault away from themselves and onto other causes.

IMPLICATIONS

This chapter has attempted to review various factors which might mediate the victim's recovery from sexual assault. The major purpose was to increase the clinician's awareness of such factors during assessment, treatment planning, implementation, and evaluation. Of special importance appears to be the victim's preassault history—her prior psychological functioning and prior life stresses, including victimization experiences—the victim's social support network, and the victim's own cognitive and behavioral coping strategies.

Chapter 4
Crisis Intervention

Relatively few victims seek treatment immediately following rape. During the initial crisis period, lasting from a few days to 2 or even 3 months postassault, women typically are not ready to engage in a treatment program that requires extended time and focused involvement. Their lives are disrupted and their overall distress is such that concentration may be difficult. Therapeutic intervention during this period is usually brief and follows a crisis counseling model. The role of the therapist is more active, directive, and supportive than that found in more traditional therapies.

Crisis intervention differs from the treatment strategies presented in subsequent chapters in a number of ways. The length of time in treatment is brief and frequently limited to one session only. The goals of crisis intervention are also limited to what can reasonably be accomplished within a short time period. Thus, it is unreasonable to expect complete resolution of the assault and its aftermath. Instead, the therapist works to reduce the victim's emotional distress, enhance her coping strategies, and prevent the development of more serious psychopathology.

In the following sections we will present some of the specific goals of crisis intervention with recent sexual assault victims. Included under each goal are suggested strategies for implementing or achieving the goal. The areas discussed are not intended to be exhaustive but are presented to acquaint the reader with those most frequently selected in crisis intervention with sexual assault victims. Several others have also written on crisis therapy in general (e.g., Butcher & Maudal, 1976) and with rape victims specifically (Burgess & Holmstrom, 1979; Kilpatrick & Veronen, 1983; Kilpatrick, Veronen, & Resick, 1982; Koss & Harvey, 1987).

METHODS OF CRISIS
INTERVENTION

Establish a Therapeutic Relationship

Establishment of a therapeutic relationship is just as critical to success with crisis intervention as it is to other therapeutic interventions; however, it may be more difficult because the duration of treatment and, thus, the contact with the victim is so brief. The therapist must be skilled at establishing rapport and communicating effectively with the victim. Both verbal and nonverbal strategies must be used to convey understanding and acceptance of the victim's recent experiences. It is important to listen attentively to the victim and show sensitivity and respect for her as a person. Emotional support should include realistic reassurance and a sense of optimism or expectation for recovery in relation to the assault and its impact on the victim.

Encourage Expression of Emotions

Most victims during the crisis period are in a state of heightened arousal and, as a result, are already motivated to discuss their experiences with minimal encouragement. In fact, the victim may repeatedly describe her assault and events surrounding the assault. The therapist must recognize the victim's need to tell and retell her experiences as therapeutic and listen attentively. As the victim talks, it is important to focus more on the victim's emotions and feelings, both during the assault and now, than on specific details within the assault, and to encourage expression of these emotions. As the victim relates her experiences, the therapist should watch for maladaptive cognitions concerning her role in the assault and her feelings of self-worth and provide support and reassurance where appropriate to challenge these beliefs and substitute more adaptive ones.

Provide Factual Information

Victims need to be provided with factual information concerning the most frequently experienced symptoms following assault, their expected intensity and duration, and the impact these symptoms can have on the victim's daily role functioning. The victim should be told that at times she may be fearful or anxious, that she may have frequent crying spells, and that she may have difficulty concentrating or experience intrusive thoughts about the assault. In addition, she may have problems with her appetite and sleeping. The victim should also be given information concerning how her symptoms should change and decrease over the next few months and be encouraged to seek professional help if she feels her recovery is prolonged or exacerbated. Reassurance that the victim's symptoms are similar to those commonly experienced by other victims helps to reduce the victim's distress over the symptoms she is exhibiting and helps to restore the victim's view of herself as normal.

Because of the victim's current level of distress, it may be difficult for her to attend to or absorb all of this information or even the parts that are most relevant to her own experiences. As a result, it may be helpful to provide the victim with written information concerning assault reactions and encourage her to read it and share it with significant others in her social network.

The victim should also be provided with factual information about rape and a discussion of some of the more common cultural myths about rape. The information presented should be relevant to the victim's assault and individualized to her own situation so that she is not overwhelmed with unhelpful facts. Carefully exploring the victim's own attitudes and beliefs about her assault and assault in general can help to identify misconceptions and potentially harmful thoughts which can then be challenged with factual information.

Anticipate Future Problems

As part of the presentation of the psychological sequelae following rape, some discussion of potential problem areas needs to be included. The victim's overall activity level, her daily role functioning, her interpersonal relationships, and her sexual functioning may all be adversely affected following rape.

Initially the victim needs to be given permission to reduce her activities in a number of areas but also encouraged to work gradually toward resuming normal functioning. The victim should be provided with a reasonable time frame to expect to return to normal and encouraged to seek professional help if problems are encountered. Discussion of coping strategies successfully used by other victims to resume normal functioning is important to provide the victim with practical ways to deal with problem areas. Coping strategies such as deep breathing and muscle relaxation should be reviewed. Teaching the victim to break difficult activities into small steps and to expose herself gradually to anxiety-provoking situations can also be helpful. Helping the victim anticipate and prepare to cope successfully with problematic situations that are likely to occur also serves to facilitate her recovery indirectly by increasing her own self-confidence and feelings of control.

Adjust Immediate Role Responsibilities

Because of the emotional distress experienced by most victims during the crisis period following sexual assault, victims may be unable to continue to function effectively in their daily roles both within and outside the family. The responsibility for caring for a home and children may create additional stress for the victim so that her recovery is delayed. Exploration with the victim of various ways in which she can reduce these responsibilities, perhaps through the help of friends and relatives, for a short time may be beneficial. Similarly, a short time away from the demands and responsibilities of work and/or school is also recommended. Again, the therapist can explore with the victim how best to accomplish this.

While it is often beneficial to reduce a victim's role responsibilities for a short time period following assault so that she has more time and energy to attend to her own needs and recovery, caution is necessary so that maladaptive behavior patterns do not develop. Some daily structure and activity is needed and regular social contacts should be maintained. Helping the victim arrive at a reasonable time frame and plan for gradually resuming role responsibilities is therefore also needed. Facilitating mastery of daily role functioning also increases a victim's sense of control and benefits her overall recovery.

Identify and Mobilize Social Support

Perhaps one of the most important tasks of crisis intervention with victims of sexual assault is the therapist's ability to facilitate the important role that friends and relatives can have in victim recovery. Many victims are reluctant to confide in significant others about the sexual assault. Discussion of the victim's concerns and her expected reactions from others is usually necessary. It is critical to help the victim confide in others appropriately so that their response is supportive. This may range from discussion of various approaches to take to actual notification by the therapist.

In mobilizing social support for the victim, it is important for the therapist to realize that the sexual assault represents a crisis for the victim but also for her friends and family. If possible, it is desirable to spend some time directly interacting with the victim's significant others. Friends and relatives may have a difficult time responding appropriately to the victim because of their own attitudes and beliefs about sexual assault. In addition, they may experience elevated levels of distress (e.g., symptoms of fear, anxiety, depression) in response to the assault, and their own emotional needs may make them less sensitive to the needs of the victim. They need to have information on what reactions to expect in the victim and themselves and ways in which they can facilitate recovery (e.g., express positive affect toward the victim, encourage expression of and validate victim feelings, reassure victim).

Discussion of potential problems with intimacy and sexual functioning with both the victim and her partner is also important. Both need to have realistic expectations concerning sexual relations and frequently encountered problems, permission to avoid sexual intercourse or specific sexual behaviors for a time, and specific strategies for resuming sexual relations.

Anticipating for the victim that her social network may at some point become impatient with her need to discuss the assault and the length of time it typically takes to recover is also important. Planning for appropriate ways to handle this should it occur and/or alternative sources of support may be helpful.

Interface with Medical and Law Enforcement Agencies

Many victims, especially relatively young ones, may be reluctant to seek appropriate medical services. It is important to ask a victim if she has seen a physician since the assault. If not, reasons for seeking medical treatment should be presented and the victim's concerns about the procedures discussed. Physical injuries, even minor tears and bruises, should receive medical care. Information concerning the possibility of sexually transmitted diseases (including AIDS) and pregnancy should be presented. Depending on the time elapsed since the assault, medical services may also be necessary for the collection of forensic evidence. Because many victims experience somatic symptoms, such as pelvic pain, it is often helpful to receive reassurance from a physician that there are no signs of internal injuries.

Many adolescent victims have little knowledge of or experience with pelvic examinations. These procedures should be discussed carefully and feelings and emotions typically experienced by victims anticipated. If possible, arrangements should be made to have a victim advocate present during the medical procedures.

Many victims may also be indecisive concerning reporting the assault to the police or have unrealistic expectations concerning the effects of such a report. The victim should be provided with information concerning the procedures involved in reporting an assault, subsequent activities such as viewing mug shots and live line-ups, and testifying in court. For victims who are opposed to reporting their assault the possibility of an anonymous report should be explored. This procedure provides law enforcement authorities with information that may be used in solving other assaults or preventing future ones. Other victims may have unrealistic expectations concerning the likelihood that the assailant will be apprehended, charged, tried, and convicted. Discussion of all possible outcomes and the victim's reactions and feelings concerning each may help her develop a realistic view of the legal outcome of her assault.

Explore Perceptions of Personal Safety

During the first few days and weeks following sexual assault, a victim may understandably have extreme fears concerning her own physical safety. Exploration of ways in which the victim can increase her feelings of safety and security are needed. Some victims are financially able to install additional locks and/or security systems or move to a safer residence or neighborhood. However, most victims lack the financial resources to accomplish major changes and other, more practical, alternatives must be determined. Some victims move in with friends of relatives for a short time or arrange for someone to stay with them.

Characteristics of the assault may influence specific safety needs. For example, if the assault occurred at or near work, arrangements to increase personal security in those locations are needed. Similarly, if the assailant was known to the victim, ways to avoid or reduce the possibility of contact with him should be developed.

Arrange for Follow-up

There are a number of possibilities concerning follow-up contact with sexual assault victims. Scheduling a second appointment in a few days is frequently desirable. However, the likelihood that the victim will keep subsequent appointments is low. Obtaining permission to contact the victim by telephone is a more feasible alternative. Providing the victim with the therapist's name and number and encouraging her to call if she has difficulties or concerns is also recommended.

Through follow-up contact the therapist can evaluate the victim's current functioning and recovery and make recommendations for subsequent contact or referral. However, as noted at the beginning of this chapter, crisis intervention is often limited to one contact. Follow-up is often hindered by the victim moving, changing telephone numbers, or leaving town for a while. In addition, many victims and their families may decide to avoid talking or thinking about the assault and decline follow-up contacts. The therapist may encourage the victim to continue treatment, but should be sensitive to the victim's wishes and fully respect her desire to discontinue contact.

Brief Behavioral Intervention Procedure

Kilpatrick, Veronen, and Resick (1982) developed a two-session, 4-hour cognitive-behavioral treatment package for use with recent rape victims. The treatment package combines elements of rape crisis counseling and stress inoculation training and is called the Brief Behavioral Intervention Procedure (BBIP).

During the first component of the BBIP, the victim is asked to describe her rape experience. As with the preceding crisis intervention strategies, the therapist acknowledges and encourages the victim's expression of feelings and emotions concerning the assault, accepts and respects the victim's experience and does not question or challenge it, and encourages the victim to view her feelings and behavior during the assault as understandable and reasonable. The second and third components of the BBIP provide the victim with (a) information concerning rape myths, (b) information about the kinds of rape-related problems they are likely to experience, and (c) a conceptualization of the development of rape-related problems. The final component of the BBIP describes various skills for coping with fear and anxiety. These include: (a) deep breathing and relaxation, (b) guided self dialogue, and (c) strategies for diminishing avoidance behavior.

Crisis intervention with recent rape victims has not been evaluated empirically. While it is intuitively appealing, its effects on length of recovery and prevention of more serious psychopathology have yet to be determined. Evaluation of specific treatment components or victim characteristics and their relation to outcome effectiveness is also needed.

CASE EXAMPLE

Nancy is an 18-year-old female. She is in her first semester at a large state university and shares an apartment with two other female college students. She had been raped one week prior to seeking help. At the time of her initial referral, she was accompanied by her boyfriend, Dave, and one roommate, Debbie.

Presenting Complaint

At her initial visit Nancy appeared tired and upset. She reported that at times she felt like she was going crazy; vivid images of the assault kept intruding into her thoughts and she would start to shake and cry uncontrollably. She had tried going to classes but had been unable to sit through even a 1-hour class. She was also unable to concentrate on schoolwork even when her roommates were with her in their apartment. At night she had difficulty falling asleep and, when she finally did, she would awaken in a few hours with terrifying nightmares of the assault.

History of Sexual Assault

The assault had occurred 1 week ago. Nancy was alone in her apartment studying for a midterm the next day. Her two roommates had gone to the library. When the doorbell rang she was surprised to see Philip, a young man who was in her roommate Shelia's math class. She explained that Sheila was at the library. Instead of leaving as she expected, Philip asked if he minded if he studied at her apartment because things were too noisy at his dorm. Nancy let him in and went back to her desk.

After some time Philip initiated a conversation with Nancy. Soon he began to talk about her and her boyfriend Dave and asked what they did on dates. Nancy became uncomfortable as his questions became more personal. Philip began to be more hostile and insulting and insisted that she and Dave were having sex together. She vigorously denied this and demanded that he leave. As he moved closer and closer to her, Philip became more verbally abusive and stated that he knew she slept with a lot of men. Nancy protested that she was a virgin and again demanded that he leave. At that point Philip grabbed her and said that she was going to have sex with him before he would leave. He pushed her into one of the bedrooms. She struggled but he threw her on the bed. When she started to scream he choked her and then put a pillow over her head to quiet her. While he raped her he made remarks insisting that she was enjoying it. Before leaving Philip threatened her that if she told anyone he would swear that she had seduced him.

After Philip left, Nancy sat on her bed and sobbed uncontrollably, rocking back and forth. Around midnight her roommates returned. When she told them what had happened they were supportive. They accompanied her to the college health center where she was treated for vaginal bleeding and lacerations. Saying she was too confused and exhausted, Nancy refused to talk to the crisis intervention worker at the health center. Although the university police were notified, Nancy also refused to talk with the law enforcement officer because she felt she needed more time to sort things out for herself.

Intervention

Initially the therapist let Nancy do most of the talking and listened attentively and provided support and reassurance. Slowly Nancy recounted the events leading up to and surrounding the assault and her difficulties over the past week.

At appropriate points the therapist introduced factual information concerning sexual assault and sexual assault myths relevant to Nancy's rape and her own beliefs and feelings. For example, Nancy was feeling guilty and angry with herself for initially trusting Philip and letting him in her apartment. The therapist pointed out that at least half of all assaults are committed by persons familiar to the victim and that there was no way that Nancy could have predicted that Philip was going to assault her. The therapist also reassured Nancy that her feelings and behavior during the assault were both understandable and reasonable given the situation. To further support this, the therapist was careful not to say anything that Nancy might interpret as questioning or challenging her behavior the night of the assault.

As Nancy talked about the assault, the therapist also watched for statements which might indicate changes in her feelings of self-worth as a result of the assault. At several points in the interview Nancy stated, "I'm too naive and trusting to be on my own"; "I'll never make it in college"; and "My judgment is so bad my parents ought to make me live at home." With each statement, the therapist acknowledged Nancy's feelings but also gently challenged and reframed the statement into a more adaptive one.

Nancy was also distraught over her inability to control her emotions and feelings since the assault. The therapist explained that the symptoms Nancy was experiencing were normal following sexual assault and most victims experienced similar reactions. She also reassured her that with time these symptoms would diminish and that she would gradually start to feel like her former self. The therapist taught Nancy techniques to induce deep muscle relaxation, and Nancy practiced these during the interview when she became upset. In addition, Nancy learned and practiced several self-statements she could make to counteract intrusive thoughts.

Because Nancy had missed two midterms during the past week, the therapist arranged for her to receive medical excuses so that she could take them at a later date. After some discussion, the therapist also contacted Nancy's dean to arrange for her to withdraw from one of her courses without penalty so that she could have a reduced course load the rest of the semester.

Nancy was terrified that she would see Philip again. This fear seemed to be the major impediment to returning to classes. Nancy and the therapist worked out a procedure so that one of Nancy's roommates or her boyfriend would accompany her to each class and meet her at the end of class. Initially Nancy was to try this with one class only but agreed that by the end of the week she would try to attend all three of her remaining classes. For the second week Nancy was to continue going to her classes accompanied by her friends but to try walking farther and farther away from them until she felt comfortable walking alone. The therapist and Nancy also discussed and role-played what Nancy would do if she did encounter Philip on campus.

Nancy was afraid to stay alone in her apartment even during the day. Because Nancy felt that moving was impossible, the therapist focused on ways to increase Nancy's feelings of safety in the apartment. Nancy's boyfriend had already purchased a can of mace, and Nancy now kept it on her person all the time when she was in the apartment. At the therapist's suggestion, Nancy agreed to have a better lock installed and a peep hole added to the front door. The therapist also discussed with Nancy the possibility of changing bedrooms with one of her roommates and the possibility of rearranging the furniture in the apartment and adding some new posters and/or plants so that it seemed like a different place.

Nancy reported that she had no difficulty discussing the assault with her roommates and her boyfriend and that all three had been supportive. However, she was conflicted about telling her parents. Not only would they be alarmed about what had happened her first time away from home, but they would insist that she withdraw from school immediately and return home. The therapist and Nancy discussed the pros and cons of telling her parents and role-played several ways of approaching her parents. Nancy was still uncertain about how best to proceed, so the therapist and Nancy agreed to postpone this decision until a later meeting.

Near the end of the session the therapist asked Nancy if her roommate and boyfriend could join them. With her consent, the therapist discussed Nancy's reactions and what to expect over the next few months. The therapist also praised their support and emphasized how important this was to Nancy's recovery. With the therapist's help, Nancy was able to ask them for the practical assistance she needed with class attendance and feeling safer in the apartment.

Before terminating the session, the therapist arranged to contact Nancy by phone the next evening and scheduled a follow-up appointment for 1 week later. The therapist also gave Nancy her phone number and encouraged her to call if some of the strategies they had planned did not work.

Chapter 5

Assessment of Nonrecent Victims

Essential to the development of an appropriate treatment plan or case disposition is an adequate assessment. Individual reactions to sexual assault vary widely and are influenced by a number of factors. Many victims show multiple problems, and the effectiveness of the treatment approach chosen may depend on a thorough understanding of this complexity. The therapist must ascertain the relationship of presenting problems to a rape trauma. Some victims may identify their presenting problems as resulting from a sexual assault, but it is more common that victims fail to seek treatment until later when problems may have become disassociated in the victim's mind with the assault itself. For that reason it is important to make assessment for a history of sexual assault a routine part of intakes. Even when asked directly, victims may not be comfortable revealing a sexual assault. In other cases, a victim's need to avoid the feelings associated with the trauma may be so strong that recall of the event is not immediately possible. Therefore, the therapist must be alert to signs of an undisclosed or unrecalled sexual assault. These include, but are not limited to: PTSD symptomatology, borderline personality disorder symptomatology, chronic anxiety, sexual dysfunctions, distrust (especially of men), chronic depression, or combinations of these. Sexual assault victims may show a wide range of problems and individual variations in the patterns of these symptoms. There is no single set of indicators that have as yet been identified. Therefore, a comprehensive assessment is essential, including a careful interview, selected paper and pencil measures as needed, and observational or physiological measures if appropriate and feasible.

INTERVIEW

In any general intake interview it is important to screen for a history of sexual assault and abuse, as well as for other forms of criminal victimization. It cannot be assumed that clients will report such events spontaneously, as shown by a study that compared rates of reporting spontaneously with rates in response to specific questions (Saunders, Kilpatrick, Resnick, & Tidwell, 1989). In this community mental health center sample, sexual assault was reported less than one third as often when clients were not questioned about it specifically (13.3% vs. 41.7%). The sexual assault screening questions used in the Saunders et al. (1989) study are reproduced in Table 5.1, along with the introductory comments that preceded them. Clinical judgment and sensitivity must be used in introducing these topics. A single question that uses the term *rape* is not advisable since many victims, especially of acquaintance rape, do not label their experiences in that way.

If, for some reason, screening is not feasible during the intake interview, the therapist might consider as part of a psychometric battery the Sexual Experiences Survey (Koss & Oros, 1982). This brief questionnaire asks about a variety of unwanted sexual experiences under varying levels of coercion. It takes only a few minutes to complete and does not require that a victim label her experience as rape in order to answer the questions.

Although a variety of standardized measures may be used, the interview remains the primary source of information and provides the opportunity for establishing a therapeutic relationship. Building rapport with rape victims can be problematic because they are often distrustful of others as a result of their experiences. They may also be hypersensitive to any indication of blame or lack of sensitivity on the part of the interviewer. Therefore, the therapist must be nonjudgmental and avoid attempting to determine whether a "real" rape occurred or whether the victim precipitated the assault in any way. A frequent question is whether or how much to focus on information concerning the assault incident itself. It is usually not necessary to go into detail about the incident. Sometimes a victim's specific reactions are better understood if this information is known, but it is rarely essential. A more appropriate time to obtain such information is after rapport has been established. The therapist should be alert to the victim's readiness to discuss the assault. In doing so the victim may become emotional and distressed and must be able to trust the therapist's ability to cope with that level of emotionality. If the assault is discussed, it is best to focus not on the sexual aspects

Table 5.1. Sexual Screening Questions

One type of event that happens to men as well as women, and boys as well as girls, is sexual mistreatment or sexual assault. Men are assaulted under the same kinds of situations as women, but it may be more difficult for a man to report an assault because he may be ashamed or fear that others will ridicule or not believe him. When asked about sexual abuse or mistreatment, many people tend to think about incidents in which they were attacked or mistreated by a total stranger. As you answer these questions, please remember that we need to know about all incidents of sexual abuse or mistreatment, not just those involving a stranger. Thus, please don't forget to tell us about incidents that might have happened when you were a child or those in which the person who tried to abuse or mistreat you was someone you knew, such as a friend, boyfriend/girlfriend, or even a spouse or family member. Here are some questions about some of these experiences you might have had.

1. Has anyone ever tried to make you have sexual relations with them against your will?

Yes, has	1
No, has not	2
Not sure	3
Refused	4

2. Has anyone *ever attempted* to rape you or *actually* raped you?

Yes, has	1
No, has not	2
Not sure	3
Refused	4

3. Have you ever had any other experience in which someone tried to molest you sexually—that is, they made serious unwanted sexual advances but did not attempt full sexual relations?

Yes, have had	1
No, haven't had	2
Not sure	3
Refused	4

4. Have you ever been in a situation in which you were pressured into doing more sexually than you wanted to do; that is, a situation in which someone pressured you against your will into forced contact with the sexual parts of your body or their body?

Yes	1
No	2
Not sure	3
Refused	4

5. Briefly describe what happened.

_____

_____

_____

Thank you.

Note. From "Brief Screening for Lifetime History of Criminal Victimization at Mental Health Intake" by B. E. Saunders, D. G. Kilpatrick, H. S. Resnick and R. P. Tidwell, 1989, *Journal of Interpersonal Violence, 4,* pp. 267–277. Copyright 1989 by Sage Publications. Reprinted by permission.

but on the victim's feelings at the time, as suggested by Koss and Harvey (1987).

Current Functioning

The victim's current functioning, including mental status, should be assessed during the interview. It is common for victims to be emotional and to have difficulties in concentration during the weeks following the assault. More serious or lasting mental status problems may reflect a preexisting condition rather than a reaction to the assault alone.

Other aspects of current functioning that should be investigated during the interview include the following: avoidance behavior; anxiety problems, including obsessive-compulsive problems, phobias, and panic attacks; paranoid ideation; depression, including suicidal ideation; other emotional problems, especially anger/aggression control difficulties; alcohol and drug use or abuse; somatic problems, whether stress related or chronic; and sexual adjustment. Sexual functioning is a sensitive area and considerable trust may need to be established prior to examining it. The relevant information includes whether the victim is currently sexually active and with what frequency, her interest and desire, level of arousal, and general satisfaction. Sexual problems to be assessed include any specific dysfunctions, especially arousal problems, painful intercourse, and any physical problems. The relationship within which the sexual behavior occurs is also important. A trusted partner who allows the victim to initiate behaviors as she feels ready can be important in establishing or reestablishing adequate sexual functioning.

Current Resources

It is important to assess the current resources or strengths the victim has at her disposal. These include coping skills, economic resources or lack thereof, and the diversity of roles or areas of achievement that contribute to her self-esteem. It is also important to assess the victim's social support system: her social network and potential sources of social support that she may not currently be using. Social support stems not only from the number of people in whom the victim feels she can confide but also the level of closeness she feels to each and the positiveness of their response to her. If there appears to be a lack of social support, this should be pursued further and the victim's level of social skills should be assessed as well as her possible avoidance of social interactions. Relationships with family and friends may have been disrupted by the assault and victims may not have found the strength to establish new ones.

History

Assessment of the victim's functioning history may be brief or more extended, depending on the circumstances. The assessment should at least touch on the history of any previous psychiatric problems, especially suicidal ideation or suicide attempts and the related risk factors. It should include previous treatment history as well as a history of prior traumatic experiences such as child abuse, battering, or previous criminal victimization. Other life crises in the recent history should also be examined as these may predispose the victim to poorer adjustment. A history of alcohol or drug abuse may predispose her to substance abuse in the current crisis. Previous sexual functioning should also be assessed, especially if current problems are indicated. It is a good idea to assess the highest previous level of functioning including education and occupation. Current level of socioeconomic functioning may not reflect accurately a victim's potential if she has made a poor adjustment following a traumatic event. Economic loss is a common consequence of sexual assault and can be severe and chronic in cases where the victim is unable to resume her previous occupation or level of work productivity. For example, one victim of a brutal assault attempted to resume her job as a schoolteacher after taking a few weeks off to recover. She found herself to be tearful, unable to concentrate, and overwhelmed when faced with minor discipline problems. Standing in front of the room produced intrusive thoughts that everyone could tell she was different, "ruined," and that they all knew what had happened to her. With the support of her principal and other teachers, she managed to complete the term but took a leave of absence the following year and was never able to return to teaching. When interviewed 15 years later, she was working part time as a maid, barely subsisting, and had lost contact with all her former friends. She had sought treatment on two or three occasions, but found it unhelpful, consisting of tranquilizing medication and little else.

Coping with the Assault

How the victim is dealing with the aftermath of the assault should be assessed from practical, legal, and emotional viewpoints, depending on the recency of the assault. Assuming that the victim is beyond the immediate crisis phase, relevant issues for assessment would include whether she has overcome any physical injuries suffered, the legal status of the case if it was reported, effects of dealing with the criminal justice system, and financial consequences the victim may have suffered.

Assessment of emotional and cognitive levels of coping should include the victim's cognitions about the assault, her current appraisal of the

situation, the meaning it currently has for her, as well as her self-perceptions and how these may have changed since the assault. Specific coping
strategies she is using to deal with the cognitions and emotions should be
assessed as well as their effectiveness. Burgess and Holmstrom (1979a)
discussed a variety of coping strategies used by rape victims. These include
(a) identifying a reason or cause that is logical to the victim (which may
or may not include self-blame); (b) dramatizing, that is, repeatedly relating
the assault to significant others and overexpressing anxiety and other
feelings; and (c) suppressing the memory of the assault. The third strategy
is often ineffective, and in assessing the victim's use of it the therapist
should assess the frequency of intruding thoughts and feelings. Complete
suppression is rare, and the feelings are usually revealed in indirect ways
(through nightmares, unexplained fears or hostilities, etc.). A fourth strategy that Burgess and Holmstrom discussed is maladaptive coping, such as
alcohol and drug use, promiscuity, and suicidal ideation, all of which
should be assessed.

We have found a semistructured format useful in interviewing sexual
assault victims. (See the Appendix for an example of this interview format.) It ensures that major areas are not overlooked but is flexible enough
to adapt easily to individual cases. Irrelevant topic areas can be deleted and
important ones explored in greater depth. The semistructured format is
used in combination with relevant written assessment instruments to give
an overview of current functioning and rape-related changes, not for formal diagnosis. It should be used flexibly and with sensitivity. For example,
if a victim is not prepared to label her experience as rape, her own terminology should be substituted. As planning for treatment progresses, more
detailed information will be needed about specific problem areas, factors
in the environment that might maintain problems, and so forth.

The Structured Clinical Interview for DSM-III-R (SCID; Spitzer, Williams, Gibbon, & First, 1988) has been used with victims, especially when
a DSM-III-R diagnosis is desired. It is a comprehensive guide to differential
diagnosis. Some training and experience are recommended prior to its use.
Several versions are available for use with inpatient, outpatient, and non-
patient populations. One version, the SCID-II, is designed for evaluation
of personality disorders.

PSYCHOMETRIC MEASURES

In addition to a thorough interview, a complete assessment includes
other cognitive behavioral and physiological measures. Typically, these are
selected as needed to confirm or to explore areas covered in the interview.
They may be used to help determine the severity of certain problems, to
aid in making diagnoses, and in treatment planning.

We will review briefly a number of psychometric instruments that have been used with rape victims. This is not a comprehensive list, but includes the measures we and others have found useful. Few instruments have been developed specifically for assessment of rape reactions. For the most part, existing measures have been used and will, therefore, not be described in detail here. Assessment for PTSD presents special problems and is covered in a separate section.

While any number of standardized general measures can be used with rape victims, published reports show that most of the instruments used have been special purpose measures that focus on depression, anxiety, self-esteem, social adjustment, or other problems. One exception is the Symptom Checklist-90-Revised (SCL-90-R) (Derogatis, 1977). It has 90 items in a checklist format, is easily administered, relatively quick, and, in addition to measuring general level of distress, has a number of subscales relevant for rape victims (e.g., depression, anxiety, hostility). As a screening device, or in the event assessment must be done in a single session, it can substitute for a battery of other tests. For screening, there is a shorter version called the Brief Symptom Index. The Minnesota Multiphasic Personality Inventory [(MMPI) Hathaway & McKinley, 1941] might be useful in certain cases but takes longer to complete.

The Veronen-Kilpatrick Modified Fear Survey (MFS) (Veronen & Kilpatrick, 1980b), a widely used instrument, was adapted to assess fears of sexual assault victims. To assess rape-relevant fears, a rape subscale was added to the Fear Survey Schedule developed by Wolpe and Lang (1964). The scale consists of 120 items that are rated on a five-point Likert scale to indicate level of fear induced by each. In addition to the rape subscale, the six original categories of fear are: animal fears, tissue damage fears, classical fears, fear of failure/loss of self-esteem, social fears, and miscellaneous fears. In addition, a total fear score is derived.

This scale was factor-analyzed by Resick, Veronen, Calhoun, Kilpatrick, and Atkeson (1986). Six factors were derived that significantly differentiated victims from nonvictims. These factors overlapped with, but were not identical to, the original scales. They were (a) a vulnerability factor (reflecting fears of situations that might make a victim feel vulnerable), (b) sexual fears, (c) fears of social evaluation and failure, (d) agoraphobic fears, (e) fear of loud or unexpected noises, and (f) fear of weapons. Victims and nonvictims did not differ on two additional factors which emerged—classical fears, such as animals and thunder, and medical fears, such as blood and surgery. In this factor analysis, 20 items from the rape subscale emerged in five different factors (the majority in vulnerability, sexual, and social evaluation fear factors). Whether the original scale scores or factor scores are used, the instrument is probably most helpful in identifying specific fears that are to be targeted for treatment.

The Rape Aftermath Symptom Test: (RAST; Kilpatrick, 1988) was developed by combining items from the SCL-90-R and the MFS. One third of the items were chosen on the basis of the fact that they provided the best discrimination between victims and non-victims at 3 months post-assault. It has internal consistency of .95 and test-retest reliability of .85 for non-victims over a 10-week period.

The Speilberger State–Trait Anxiety Scale (Speilberger, Gorsuch, & Lushene, 1970) has been used in several studies of traumatic rape reactions. It has the advantage of brevity and can be used repeatedly to assess change over time.

In cases that require a detailed differential assessment of anxiety problems, the Anxiety Disorders Interview Schedule–Revised (DiNardo et al., 1985) provides a format consistent with DSM-III-R categories of anxiety disorders. Although such disorders may predate the rape trauma, all have been observed consequent to rape as well. Regardless of origin, they must be addressed in treatment.

The most frequently used depression measure is the Beck Depression Inventory [(BDI) Beck, Ward, Mendelson, Mock, & Erbaugh, 1961]. The BDI has the advantage of being brief (21 items) and has been used extensively, so norms are readily available.

The Hamilton Rating Scale for Depression (Hamilton, 1960) has been used to assess depression in victims. It is based on a structured interview and combines client responses to depression-related questions with ratings made by the interviewer from observations of client's energy level, response latency, and so forth. Although it takes longer than the BDI, it correlates highly (about .75) with it and is a good alternative when there is reason to suspect the accuracy of self-report.

The Profile of Mood States (McNair, Lorr, & Droppleman, 1971) is a good measure of mood changes. It can be used to track treatment progress or to assess current mood state. It is a relatively brief, 65-item, adjective rating scale that measures six mood factors, all of which have relevance for rape victims: tension/anxiety, depression, fatigue, vigor, anger/hostility, and confusion.

Although indications of self-esteem problems are often observed in rape victims, few standardized measures have been used. The Tennessee Self-Concept Scale [(TSCS) Fitts, 1965] is one exception. It provides an overall self-esteem score as well as a number of specific self-concept scores (e.g., social, physical, family). It appears to be sensitive to changes, and so can be useful as a measure of treatment outcome. However, it is not brief (100 items) and the scoring is somewhat complicated.

The Self-Report Inventory (Bown & Richek, 1967) is another measure of self-esteem that has been found to differentiate rape victims and non-victims. It includes eight subscales that reflect self-esteem in various areas such as work, family, and hope for the future, and is briefer (48 items) than the TSCS.

The Rosenberg Self-Esteem Scale (Rosenberg, 1965) can be used as a brief screening measure if no detailed information about areas of self-esteem is desired. With only 10 items, it gives a single overall score for self-esteem.

For assessment of social functioning, the Social Adjustment Scale–Self Report (Weissman & Bothwell, 1976) is typically used. It is a self-report form of a structured interview developed earlier. Functioning in several areas is assessed by self-ratings (e.g., work/school, social/leisure, family).

To assess cognitive functioning, the Impact of Events Scale (Horowitz, Wilner, & Alvarez, 1979) is recommended. Designed specifically to assess the impact of traumatic events, it can be used for either current state or change over time. It is brief (15 items) and contains two factor-analytically derived subscales that measure the most common cognitive experiences of victims, intrusion of thoughts about the trauma and avoidance of such thoughts.

Assessment of sexual functioning may require multiple measures in addition to the interview and sexual history. Frequency of sexual behavior is not a good measure because it correlates poorly with arousal and satisfaction. Depending on the types of problems identified in the interview, there are several self-report measures that might be selected. The Derogatis Sexual Functioning Inventory (Derogatis & Melisoratos, 1979) is a general measure that taps a wide variety of areas, such as sexual satisfaction, knowledge about sex, and sexual experiences. It can be used for screening prior to an interview or as an adjunct to it. The Sexual Anxiety Scale (Obler, 1973) measures sex-related anxiety among heterosexual adults and may be useful in treatment planning. The Sexual Arousability Inventory (Hoon, Hoon, & Wincze, 1976) assesses arousal related to specific stimuli and can be used with either heterosexual or homosexual adults. Becker (1983) adapted a new instrument called the Female Sexual Adjustment Scale, to assess response to sexual dysfunction therapy. It can be used regardless of partner status or sexual orientation. Becker (1983) derived five summary scales: Frequency of Sexual Interaction, Frequency of Orgasm, Sexual Satisfaction, Awareness of Arousal, and Body Satisfaction. The scales have good internal consistency and all significantly differentiated sexually dysfunctional and functional women.

For measurement of coping strategies following rape, Burt and Katz (1987, 1988) developed a set of three instruments that address coping behavior, self-perceptions, and changes related to recovery. The first, titled "How I Deal with Things," has 33 items rated on a seven-point scale. A factor analysis yielded five factors: avoidance, expressive, nervous/anxious, cognitive, and self-destructive strategies.

The second instrument, "How I See Myself Now," has 43 items that measure various components of self-concept. Six factors emerged from this scale: independence/competence, angry/needy/lonely, mental health, trust, help, and guilt/blame.

The third instrument, "Changes that Have Come from Your Efforts to Recover," which has 28 items rated on a seven-point scale of "much less" to "much more" than before the rape, had three factors: self-value, positive actions, and interpersonal skills. The Interpersonal Skills scale has several items relating to awareness of sexism as well as choosing and relying on supportive friends. Positive actions include self-confidence and self-reliance.

PSYCHOPHYSIOLOGICAL ASSESSMENT

Assessment of psychophysiological functioning can be a useful adjunct in some cases, although in many settings it may not be practical. Physiological assessment is used most often in assessing for a possible diagnosis of PTSD. Heart rate and skin conductance are the only physiological measures that have been shown reliably to discriminate between PTSD sufferers and nonsufferers. Most of the research using psychophysiological measures has been done with combat veterans and has shown physiological arousal (especially heart rate increases) in response to trauma (combat) stimuli (Gerardi, Blanchard, & Kolb, 1989). Measures other than heart rate (skin conductance, blood pressure, frontal electromyograph (EMG) have shown varying levels of ability to discriminate PTSD and non-PTSD subjects, but none did as well as heart rate. Blanchard, Kolb, Gerardi, Ryan, and Pallmayer (1986) found PTSD sufferers to have higher resting heart rates as well as higher average heart rates across experimental conditions than non-PTSD sufferers. This is indicative of the chronic hyperarousal seen in all forms of anxiety disorders (Barlow, 1988). While little research has been done on psychophysiological assessment of rape victims, existing results are consistent with those for combat veterans (Kozak, Foa, Olasov-Rothbaum, & Murdock, 1988). These measures should be used only in combination with self-report and other measures to make diagnostic decisions. They are probably most useful as pre–post measures to monitor effectiveness of treatment.

The use of psychophysiological assessment of sexual arousal has been reported in a few cases. Becker and Abel (1981) used a photoplethysmographic vaginal probe. This method may have promise since victims often report a loss of sexual responsivity and may be out of touch with their own physical arousal levels. However, the method requires specialized equipment and skills, its reliability has not been definitively demonstrated, and it may be unacceptable to many women. Therefore, its general use is not recommended, though it might be useful in specific cases, especially to track treatment progress.

ASSESSING FOR PTSD

Keeping PTSD diagnostic criteria in mind while conducting the general interview should indicate whether more specific assessment for PTSD is necessary. Co-disorders are common with PTSD, however, and making a single diagnosis is sometimes difficult. Therefore, interview questions relating specifically to the major criteria are usually warranted with sexual assault victims. These include reexperiencing phenomena, avoidance or numbing of affect, increased autonomic arousal, and some indication of the duration of such symptoms. Examples of PTSD symptoms would include such problems as excessive distress at exposure to seemingly innocuous events, intrusive thoughts or fears stemming from the event while waking, and nightmares while sleeping. Examples of avoidance or numbing could include psychogenic amnesia, restricted range of affect, diminished interest in activities, or feelings of detachment or disengagement from others and from the world at large. It has also been noted that PTSD sufferers have a foreshortened future sense. They live from day to day or minute to minute with little evidence of planning for the future (Keane, 1988). They may find it difficult to imagine a future that is less bleak than their current lives. Evidence of increased arousal would include distractibility, sleep disturbances, diffuse irritation or anger, exaggerated startle responses, and hypervigilence, which might lead PTSD sufferers to take excessive or bizarre steps to protect themselves from real or perceived dangers.

A structured interview format is recommended in addition to a mental status exam. It should cover prerape as well as postrape functioning including developmental history and prior level of coping, social, vocational, educational, and behavioral adjustment. For assessment of combat-related PTSD, the Jackson Structured Clinical Interview (Keane et al., 1985) has been developed. Parts of it may be useful for rape victims until a similar interview is developed that would reflect their unique experiences. The only structured interview published to date for noncombat-related PTSD is a subsection of the revised SCID (Spitzer et al., 1988). It focuses on current symptoms related to the diagnostic criteria and has been criticized as lacking careful documentation of pre- and posttrauma development (Wolfe et al., 1987).

A multimethod approach to assessment of PTSD is important. Even though little has been published regarding norms for sexual assault victims, use of multiple instruments adds to confidence in a diagnosis. More work has examined norms for combat-related PTSD, and these point to several useful instruments. The MMPI (Hathaway & McKinley, 1941) is the most studied. Several studies have supported its utility for discriminating combat-related PTSD. The typical profile is a high F scale and a 2-8/8-2 profile. Keane, Malloy, and Fairbank (1984) developed a subscale of the MMPI for the assessment of PTSD in combat veterans. We have found this scale useful with noncombat trauma victims as well, though the scores are often less elevated.

Several other aforementioned instruments frequently used with rape victims have been found to contribute to a diagnosis of PTSD. These include the Spielberger State-Trait Anxiety Inventory, the BDI and the Social Adjustment Self-Report Scale. The Impact of Event Scale is useful because it measures two of the most salient features of PTSD, intrusive cognitions and numbing of affect. The SCL-90 also includes many items relevant to PTSD symptoms and a crime-related PTSD scale has been developed (Saunders, Mandoki & Kilpatrick, in press). It has internal consistency of .93 and correctly classified 89% of cases.

CASE CONCEPTUALIZATION

All the information gathered in assessment should be integrated, inconsistencies resolved, and an individual formulation of the case developed. This should be discussed with the victim as a prelude to a discussion of treatment goals and plans. We usually present a tentative formulation, solicit the victim's input and clarify questions, and then refine the formulation using her feedback. Treatment targets should be obvious from the formulation, but setting specific goals and how and in what order to approach them should be decided in full partnership with the victim. For treatment to be effective, the goals must be hers and she must understand and accept fully the purpose of the treatment methods used. If the case has been assessed and conceptualized properly, treatment goals and methods will follow naturally. However, flexibility is important in implementing treatment and in the formulation as well. No assessment can cover everything, and new information emerges during the course of treatment. As it does, it should be incorporated into the formulation. If it is inconsistent with the original picture, the formulation may need to be changed. This in turn can affect the approach to treatment.

Having a clear, coherent conceptualization serves as a guide to treatment and eliminates trial and error. When the victim understands her own case formulation as thoroughly as the therapist and sets her own goals, her active involvement in treatment increases. Theoretical models that help to explain the development and maintenance of rape-induced problems should be incorporated into discussions of how the individual case is conceptualized. These are described in later chapters. In addition, we usually find it helpful to give victims factual information about rape, especially incidence data and common reactions. This helps to normalize their own experience and reassure them about their reactions, so that their attention can be shifted to more positive coping measures.

Chapter 6

Treatment of Fear and Anxiety

Fear and anxiety reactions are among the most pervasive as well as the most enduring problems faced by victims of sexual assault. The assault situation is often a life-threatening one and even when no death threats are made or weapon used, a victim often perceives herself to be in danger of death or serious injury. This traumatic situation results in a state of generalized anxiety that usually lasts for several weeks and in many cases much longer. Several longitudinal studies have documented fear and anxiety reactions that, in some cases, last for years. During the initial period following the assault, most victims experience extreme anxiety, feelings of vulnerability, and nightmares. Flashbacks and panic may be brought on by any exposure to assault-related cues. Victims frequently respond by attempting to protect themselves from frightening associations. This leads to avoiding any situations that are frightening for them, and their avoidance attempts can lead to greater disruptions in their lives. For example, they frequently move or change jobs. They may restrict their activities to avoid meeting new people or getting into situations where they feel vulnerable. Restricting activities can contribute to depression. Longer term problems can include the development of specific phobias and obsessive-compulsive behavior such as checking rituals.

Victims vary considerably in the pattern of fears they show, and it is important for treatment planning that these individual differences be assessed. Situational factors in the assault may determine specific fears. For example, a fear of parking lots may develop if that is where the assault occurred. Women who are assaulted in their own homes have a great deal of difficulty feeling comfortable and safe there again. They often have to move to reduce their anxiety. Over one third of rape victims show significantly elevated scores on the MFS Schedule 1 year or more following the assault. In one case a husband sought help for his wife who had become agoraphobic and had not left the house for 2 years following a sexual assault. Debilitating fears have been observed in some victims many years later. Why some victims are able to make a more rapid recovery than others in the absence of treatment is a question still under study. The answer does not seem to lie in the assault itself. Assault characteristics such as presence or absence of a weapon, location of the assault, or whether the assailant is known to the victim have not been found consistently to predict severity of later reactions. One reason for this seems to be that almost all assaults are subjectively experienced by the victim as life threatening. Another reason may be the confounding effects of pre-assault functioning and predispositions.

Social learning theory explanations for the development of fear and anxiety responses in victims of sexual assault have provided the conceptualization underlying most treatment approaches to date. In this model, a single experience of a traumatic nature is seen as sufficient to produce a classically conditioned fear response, especially in individuals predisposed physiologically and/or who have been exposed in the past to fearful models. The tendency to avoid or escape feared situations and objects reinforces the fear and prevents its extinction. In addition, the fear can generalize to cues similar to those in the initial situation or, through higher order conditioning, to apparently unrelated cues. Thus, some victims, long after the assault, do not realize that their anxiety problems are connected with the rape experience and therefore fail to inform the therapist of that experience. Treatment may not be effective in such cases without uncovering and dealing with the rape aftermath. The importance of a thorough assessment of each case should not be minimized.

Kilpatrick and Veronen (1983) suggested that the conditioning process can include cognitive stimuli such as thoughts salient during the rape. Thus, thoughts can produce a fear response in the absence of concrete cues. In a similar way, it may be assumed that semantic generalization can occur, so that words or thoughts that become associated with conditioned stimuli produce anxiety through higher order conditioning. Kilpatrick et al. (1982) pointed out that higher order conditioning may produce avoidance of people with whom experiences and feelings about the rape have been shared, including therapists. This may help explain the behavior, commonly seen in these clients, that is sometimes labeled resistance. Because therapy has positive aspects for clients as well as evoking conditioned anxiety, an approach-avoidance conflict may be set up, resulting in missed appointments and emotionally charged behavior alternating with clear motivation for treatment. Therapists should understand this and deal with it when necessary.

More recent models for the development of anxiety disorders subsequent to trauma are based on Lang's (1979) information processing theory of fear. Lang posited that fear-relevant information is organized in memory in the form of semantic "fear networks," functionally organized sets of propositions about (a) fear-eliciting stimuli; (b) cognitive, motoric, and psychophysiological responses; and (c) the meaning such stimuli and responses take on for the individual. Those with anxiety disorders are seen to have highly organized and stable fear networks that can be activated in response to minimal cues. For any significant therapeutic change to occur, all three elements of the network must be accessed, and the information processed. Foa and Kozak (1986) and Foa, Steketee, and Olasov-Rothbaum (1989) elaborated on this model with regard to treatment and relevance for PTSD. They proposed that complete emotional processing occurs only when all three elements of the fear networks are accessed and exposed to corrective information. This corrective information must be incompatible with at least some elements of the fear network and these new elements integrated into the existing network. Therefore, corrective information is learned (e.g., anxiety diminishes with prolonged exposure).

A recent model aimed at explaining the role of cognition in PTSD is drawn from emotional processing concepts and information processing theory (Chemtob, Roitblat, Hamada, Carlson, & Twentyman, 1988). PTSD sufferers are known to be hypervigilant and overattentive to potential danger cues. Chemtob et al. suggest they are also likely to interpret ambiguous cues as threatening.

The importance of addressing the roles played by physiological, emotional, and cognitive factors is recognized in most current treatment approaches. The relative emphasis placed on each varies, but all need, directly or indirectly, to be incorporated into treatment. Ideally, the pattern of reactions shown by the individual victim should dictate how much of treatment will focus on cognitions versus emotions versus behavior. Ongoing assessment throughout treatment serves as a check on progress in each area. These can be quick and simple measures such as fear thermometers, behavioral approach tests, or recorded frequency of intrusive thoughts. Goals of treatment should include helping a victim to integrate cognitive and emotional aspects of the trauma.

TREATMENT APPROACHES

Women seeking treatment will vary in their reactions depending on a number of factors including preassault functioning, assault variables, and time since assault. Treatment should follow a careful assessment of individual problems and reactions and be tailored to the needs of a particular case. Treatment is rarely sought by victims except at one of two points in time. The first is during the initial crisis period, which may last for several weeks following the assault. The second is several months or even years later (about 2 years on average) when anxiety has failed to extinguish and the victim realizes that she is not able to function normally through her own efforts.

Avoidance and denial are normal reactions to traumatic events, but they prevent integration of the experience into the cognitive-emotional network. At some level, it remains active in memory and attempts to ignore it frequently are interrupted by intrusive thoughts and memories. To be effective, treatment must include some form of re-experiencing, which short-circuits avoidance and promotes cognitive-emotional processing of the experience. Cognitive recall alone is insufficient. Relating feelings, in itself, appears to be insufficient as well. The meaning to the individual should be addressed along with the feelings to maximize effects of treatment on behavior and physiological arousal.

Horowitz (1976), from a psychodynamic perspective, developed a brief psychotherapy emphasizing the importance of helping trauma victims reexperience the event in controlled "doses." Therapy provides a safe environment for reexperiencing memories and emotional reactions to the event as well as the cognitive distortions that may have resulted from the victim's attempts to make sense of it, which can then be confronted and restructured. A stepwise approach is used that gradually breaks through denial and emotional numbness without overwhelming the victim with intense negative emotion. A supportive therapeutic relationship as well as social support from the environment are emphasized. Little empirical research has been reported on the effectiveness of this approach. Brom, Kleber, and Defares (1989) found it equally effective as hypnotherapy and psychodynamic therapy with victims of various traumas. All were more effective than a waiting-list control group.

Systematic Desensitization

Systematic desensitization (Wolpe, 1958) has been a widely used procedure for the treatment of phobias and other anxiety problems. However, it has been used rarely with sexual assault victims. Since it is so widely known, the method will not be described here in detail. Its aim is to desensitize fear responses by eliciting them in association with responses incompatible with fear, usually relaxation. A hierarchy of fear stimuli is developed and worked through from least to most fear producing, with exposure to each item until it no longer produces anxiety. In vivo desensitization has supplanted the use of imaginal exposure, except where actual exposure is not feasible. Sexual assault victims who are not in treatment sometimes report spontaneous attempts to reach the same goal by forcing themselves gradually to approach situations of which they have developed fears resulting from rape.

Wolff (1977) reported successful treatment of fears of being alone at night and resulting insomnia in a victim of attempted rape. Only seven desensitization sessions were necessary. Turner (1979) and Frank and Stewart (1983) used systematic desensitization during the early postrape period and reported improvement in fears, assessed by self-report and behavioral change. Spontaneous recovery cannot be ruled out, however, since these were uncontrolled studies.

The use of systematic desensitization with victims is controversial. Some experts regard it as an unsuitable treatment method for sexual assault victims. Becker and Abel (1981), for example, pointed out shortcomings including its failure to teach specific generalizable skills. Further, it was designed for the treatment of irrational fears, whereas many of the fears of victims are realistic (e.g., fear of being raped again). Systematic desensitization appears to be unpopular with many victims, as well, which could result in a high dropout rate. When given a choice of treatment approaches, victims usually choose other methods (Kilpatrick & Vernonen, 1983). One reason for this may be the more passive role of the client in systematic desensitization, reminiscent of the passive role enforced during assault. Victims need to feel they are regaining active control and therefore respond better to approaches involving active coping skills.

Exposure Treatment

Exposure-based treatment methods, variously referred to as flooding or implosion, aim to break the association between anxiety and the feared cues by deliberate confrontation of feared situations until habituation occurs and the cues no longer elicit anxiety. Because avoidance is prevented, it can no longer be negatively reinforced by anxiety reduction. The client learns that her fear abates without resorting to escape. Escape and avoidance maintain anxiety at a high level, whereas exposure detaches the physiological reactions as well as the cognitive experience of fear from the cues and renders them neutral. The expectation of dire results in the face of prolonged exposure to feared situations is disproven and new cognitions and expectancies can replace old ones.

It is important in any treatment approach that the client understands the rationale and method and that she gives active consent and cooperation. This is especially true of exposure, since anxiety levels experienced by the client can be high initially. It must be made clear why this is necessary and why escape prior to habituation (e.g., premature termination of a session) will only prolong the problem. The therapist should direct sessions carefully so that anxiety is raised sufficiently for habituation but not so quickly that it is intolerable. Though it is necessary that the therapist be firm, it is equally important to be supportive and encouraging.

As in all behavioral approaches, the first step is a careful assessment of the fears. These may include objects such as weapons, situations such as being alone at night, internal images or thoughts such as may have been experienced during the rape, fears of being attacked, or things to be avoided. As a guide in treatment the victim should assign an anxiety rating to each fear (e.g., 0–100). A scene incorporating each fear should be developed for use in exposure. During each session, a scene is described and the client asked to imagine it vividly. It usually is best to start with moderately fear-provoking scenes and progress to the most fearful ones.

The length of sessions should not be arbitrarily set, since it is important to continue exposure until anxiety is reduced. Ninety-minute sessions are usually sufficient. Total reduction of anxiety may not be possible initially and does not appear necessary. The scene should be repeated at the next session and anxiety should fade more quickly. As a guide, the client should be asked to give frequent ratings of her anxiety throughout the session. A reasonable goal is approximately a 50% reduction from initial levels. If anxiety shows no signs of abating over a lengthy session, the therapist should not end the session without making sure it is declining. Suggestions to imagine mastering the fear or coping in some fashion could be used as an aid.

Instead of, or in addition to, imaginal exposure, in vivo exposure should be used whenever possible. This should follow the same guidelines as imaginal exposure. With some fears it may be faster. With others, clients need imaginal exposure first, before they can face a real situation. Homework assignments between sessions facilitate treatment. The victim may repeat imaginal scenes on her own, possibly with the aid of tapes. She may also practice in vivo exposure for scenes that have been conquered in sessions.

While flooding has been used effectively with sufferers of PTSD, notably Vietnam veterans, its use with sexual assault victims has been more limited. One concern has been that the initial high levels of anxiety might make treatment aversive and lead to premature termination. A good relationship with the victim and care in explaining the treatment should prevent this in most cases, along with more gradual exposure. Another concern is that victims might not have alternative coping strategies when avoidance is removed. This must be assessed in each case and coping skills taught when needed (see Stress Inoculation Training section). Experience with other populations has shown that it may not always be necessary.

Another criticism is that exposure treatment does not deal with irrational cognitions. The role of irrational cognitions in the etiology of rape reactions is not completely understood and it may not always be necessary to deal with them directly. Decreasing the anxiety may also affect associated negative cognitions (Rychtarik, Silverman, Van Landingham, & Prue, 1984). Exposure-based treatment has had great success with other populations, producing results rapidly. Initial results with rape victims indicate equal success. Haynes and Mooney (1975) used flooding successfully in four cases reporting fear of sexual assault, and Rychtarik et al. (1984) used it with an incest victim. Foa and colleagues have begun to report results from an ongoing outcome study of exposure treatment for rape victims (Rothbaum & Foa, 1988).

Exposure combined with response prevention (preventing anxiety, reducing avoidance responses, Meyer and Chesser, 1970) has been successful with obsessive-compulsive disorders and would be recommended in cases where sexual assault victims have developed obsessional intrusive thoughts and/or repetitive, ritualistic motor behaviors. The most common of these appear to be such behaviors as checking and rechecking locks and windows for fear of intruders. Little has been published concerning this problem with rape victims, which may indicate that it is not a common problem or that it is overshadowed by more prominent difficulties. Wolff (1977) treated a victim with checking rituals using negative practice. For 1 week she had to perform her elaborate checking ritual five distinct times upon entering her home. Thereafter, she was required to complete the checks five times in succession or not at all. The frequency quickly dropped to zero, and no further problems were seen at follow-up.

Litz, Blake, Gerardi, and Keane (1990) surveyed experts in the treatment of PTSD as to the factors they consider in judgments about when to use flooding techniques in treatment. Based on these results, they developed a decision tree that is reprinted in Figure 6.1. It assumes that a sound therapeutic alliance has been formed, the client is motivated, and a thorough assessment has been completed. Though it relates specifically to those diagnosed as suffering from PTSD, the same considerations could be applied with other forms of trauma reactions.

Exposure is often considered the treatment of choice for those with PTSD (Keane, Fairbank, Caddell, & Zimering, 1989). However, respondents to the Litz et al. (1990) survey indicated that they do not always use it. Contraindications noted included (a) comorbidity with psychosis or depression; (b) poor cognitive functioning (presumably low IQ); and (c) sometimes, concurrent character or substance abuse disorders, inability to image, and poor physical health.

Writing About the Trauma

Another procedure that can be helpful in the reexperiencing process is having victims write about the trauma. This is most useful when victims do not feel able to talk about it to a therapist or others. It also helps in cases

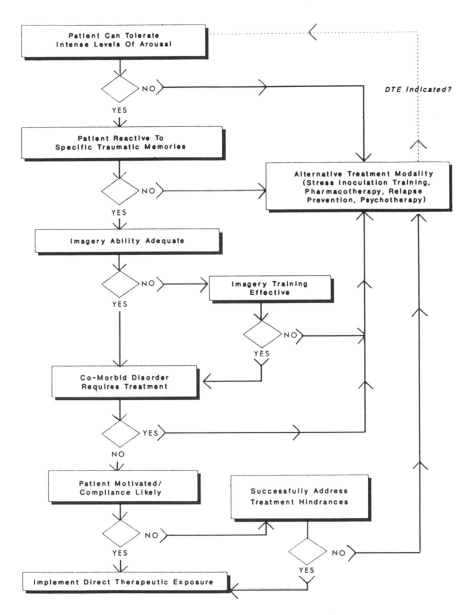

FIGURE 6.1. Decision tree for the use of direct therapeutic exposure (DTE). From "Decision Making Guidelines for the Use of Direct Therapeutic Exposure in the Treatment of Post-Traumatic Stress Disorder" by B. T. Litz, D. D. Blake, R. G. Gerardi, and T. M. Keane, 1990, *The Behavior Therapist, 13,* pp. 91–93. Copyright 1990 by the Association for Advancement of Behavior Therapy. Reprinted by permission of the publisher and the author.

where a victim feels compelled to retell her story over and over, perhaps because it facilitates cognitive integration and finding some meaning in the experience. Research on this technique has focused on its effects on physical health. Pennebaker and Beall (1986), for example, found that writing about a previous traumatic life event on 4 consecutive days resulted in decreased health center visits during a 6-month follow-up. Subjects were healthy college students. Those who wrote about both the facts of the event and their emotions improved most. Similar effects on mood have been found (Greenberg & Stone, 1989), but users should be aware that there is an initial increase in negative mood and physiological reactions such as blood pressure. This is probably due to the effects of reexperiencing emotions that have been suppressed. Clients should be prepared for this. No serious or lasting negative effects have been reported.

Research on this technique has not been extensive and has focused on physical health benefits, but it appears promising. When using it, the following points should be emphasized: (a) Writing about feelings as well as cognitions appears to be essential; (b) writing should be repeated several times (4 consecutive days is typical); and (c) the client should be told that it is her own choice whether to share what she writes with the therapist or anyone else (thus she is more likely to express herself freely). Victims often want to share what they have written, and these accounts can be useful in identifying phobic cues, distorted cognitions, and so on.

Stress Inoculation Training

Stress Inoculation Training (SIT) is the most comprehensive and well-researched treatment program that has been used with victims of sexual assault to date. Developed by Meichenbaum (1985), it was adapted for use with rape victims by Kilpatrick et al. (1982) and can be used either with individuals or with groups. It is aimed at giving a woman a sense of mastery over her fears by teaching her a variety of coping skills from which she can select when facing a fear-evoking situation.

Stress inoculation training is approached in phases. The first phase is educational in nature and provides the woman with an explanatory or conceptual framework from which she can understand the nature and origin of her fear and anxiety. This appears to be an important element in the treatment. Research has shown that victims' reactions are reduced if they have cognitive conceptual framework for understanding and making sense of the assault and its aftermath. In SIT the social learning theory explanation is used. Along with this, fear and anxiety reactions are explained as occurring along three channels (Lang, 1968): (a) the physical or autonomic channel, (b) the behavioral or motoric channel, and (c) the cognitive channel. Specific examples are given for each, and the woman is encouraged to relate her own reactions within each channel. Interrelationships among the three channels are explained and discussed.

The second phase of SIT is the training of coping skills. Two coping skills are taught for each of the three channels. The woman is asked first to select three target fears she would like to reduce. She is asked to complete an emotion thermometer on which she rates her level of fear and her level of happiness three times a day. In addition, she keeps a daily record of the number of thoughts she has regarding each target fear during each morning, afternoon, and evening.

The general format for training of coping skills is the same for all six skills taught. It includes, in sequence, a definition of the coping skill, a rationale, an explanation of the mechanism by which the skill works, a demonstration of the skill, application of the skill with a problem area that is unrelated to the target behaviors, then a review of how well the skill worked, and finally, application and practice of the skill with an example related to the target fear. Typically, skills taught for coping with fear in the physical channel are muscle relaxation and breathing control.

Muscle Relaxation. To teach muscle relaxation the Jacobsonian (1938) tension–relaxation contrast method is used most frequently. Total relaxation of all major muscle groups is included during the first training session. In addition, a tape of the relaxation session is provided for the victim to take home and use in practice assignments. Training is continued until proficiency is reached. Women are encouraged to practice their relaxation skills during everyday activities.

Breath Control. Deep diaphragmatic breathing is taught using psychocybernetics exercises. This skill is also practiced in session and at home between sessions.

For the behavioral channel, covert modeling and role-playing are the coping skills usually taught.

Covert Modeling. The woman is taught to visualize a fear or anxiety-provoking situation and imagine herself confronting it successfully. This skill is practiced until proficiency is obtained. Because people vary widely in their ability to visualize such situations, the time needed to master this skill is variable. The skill is useful in preparing for situations that a woman knows will likely produce the fear and anxiety reactions.

Role-Playing. The client and therapist act out successful coping in anxiety-producing scenes that the woman expects to be confronted with. In group situations, other group members may be used in the role-playing as well. The woman may then be asked to role-play scenes with family members or friends.

Thought Stoppage. For the cognitive channel, thought stoppage is useful in breaking up the obsessional thoughts that characterize many victims' reactions. The woman is asked to begin generating thoughts about the feared stimuli, and then those thoughts are interrupted initially by having the therapist yell, "Stop!" simultaneously clapping hands together loudly. Then the woman is asked to use the word *stop* subvocally or to devise her own covert thought-stopping term or visualization. She then learns to use thought stopping covertly and to substitute a relaxed state for the anxious state.

Guided Self-Dialogue. The woman is taught to focus on her internal dialogue and trained to label negative irrational and maladaptive self-statements. She is then taught to substitute more adaptive self-verbalizations. Following the framework of Meichenbaum (1974), self-dialogue is taught in four categories: preparation, confrontation and management, coping with feelings of being overwhelmed, and reinforcement. For each of these categories, a series of questions and/or statements are generated which encourage the woman to assess the actual probability of the negative event happening, to manage the overwhelming fear and avoidance behavior, to control self-criticism and self-devaluation, to engage in the feared behavior, and finally to reinforce herself for making the attempt and for following the steps in her training.

For each coping skill, practice assignments are given. Mild everyday stresses are confronted first in trying the coping skills. When these are mastered, the rape-related target behaviors are confronted. The client confronts each of the target behaviors she has identified in sequence. Following successful coping with the first target behavior, treatment is focused on the second. During this phase the client again completes the emotion thermometers on a daily basis. This allows the therapist to check on progress and adjust the treatment as needed.

Treatment of Nightmares and Flashbacks

Rape victims frequently suffer recurrent nightmares and flashbacks, especially in the early aftermath of the assault. In most cases, they cease after a period of time and do not require therapeutic intervention. In other cases, however, they may be so severe or lasting that treatment is requested. Typically nightmares are only one of several problems presented and their treatment should be part of a comprehensive approach.

Nightmares have not been studied enough to shed light on their etiology. But they have been found to correlate significantly with manifest anxiety (Hersen, 1971) and are commonly seen in recent victims of natural disasters and other traumas. Vietnam veterans have reported nightmares many years later. Nightmare frequency is correlated with other sleep disturbances, such as insomnia and difficulty falling asleep (Hersen, 1971). In a study of college students' nightmares, Haynes and Mooney (1975) found that the most common themes were: helplessness—47%, falling—29%, feelings of anxiety—21%, death—21%, rejection—18%, physical assault—16%. Being forced to surrender control and therefore feeling helpless is a salient feature of sexual assault, and it may be speculated that this triggers a basic, natural human fear, contributing to a tendency for these thoughts and memories to intrude into consciousness while sleeping or waking.

Nightmares are most effectively treated when conceptualized as anxiety responses. Studies of their treatment have not been numerous, and none using actual rape victims have been published to date. However, exposure-based treatment methods and systematic desensitization have both been reported to be effective in case studies of nonvictims. Geer and Silverman (1969), Cautela (1968), and Silverman and Geer (1968) used systematic desensitization to reduce frequency and intensity of nightmares. Haynes and Mooney (1975) used a form of flooding to treat four women who reported nightmare themes including fear of being raped, though all denied having been raped in actuality. After three to six 1-hour weekly sessions during which subjects were flooded with vivid descriptions of their nightmare themes, all showed significant improvement in the frequency and intensity of nightmares, and improvement continued at 3-month follow-up.

Flashbacks may be characterized as waking nightmares in that they are vivid experiences accompanied by similar physiological reactions and intense feelings of anxiety. They may be conditioned reactions triggered by something salient in the assault situation. For example, one victim experienced flashbacks upon feeling the hair on her husband's chest, because that was one of the things she recalled vividly about the assault. In some cases, however, victims may not be able to identify so specific a cue. Flashbacks seem to follow a pattern similar to nightmares in that they tend to become less frequent over time. Although no studies have been published specifically addressing the treatment of flashbacks in rape victims, it is reasonable to expect them to respond to the same general approach as nightmares. Studies of combat veterans with PTSD support the efficacy of exposure-based approaches.

Assertion Training

Assertion training is sometimes used in rape prevention programs and would appear to have value for former victims as well. Amick and Calhoun (1987) found that one of the few variables on which women who had successfully resisted sexual aggression differed from those whose resistance was unsuccessful was the Social Presence scale of the California Personality Inventory (CPI). This scale measures self-reported social poise and confidence in interpersonal interactions. Training victims in skills that enhance their confidence to handle such situations would address one of the chief fears they express—the fear of being assaulted again. Properly done, assertion training includes refining the ability to read subtle cues in another person's behavior, so the likelihood of missing danger signals in potentially risky interactions is reduced.

Another reason for using assertion training with rape victims is its potential for counterconditioning fear reactions. For rape victims, to whom being in control is important, an active counterconditioning procedure has greater appeal than a passive measure like relaxation. Given an informed choice, most victims want to learn active coping skills.

Several good guides to assertion training have been published (e.g., Lange & Jakubowski, 1976) and can be adapted readily for sexual assault victims by using relevant problems and role-play situations. Victims learn to distinguish passive, assertive, and aggressive behavior, so that they more accurately interpret the behavior of others and gain more control in their interactions. In addition, nonassertive cognitions are restructured and the right to be assertive and have one's needs respected is addressed. Assertion training can be done in either group or individual therapy.

Resick, Jordan, Girelli, Hutter, and Marhoefer-Dvorak (1988) reported a study in which three different types of group treatment were compared: stress inoculation, assertion training, and supportive psychotherapy plus information and education regarding rape reactions. All three groups improved significantly after six sessions and maintained their improvement on anxiety and assertiveness measures through a 6-month follow-up. Improvements on depression and self-esteem measures were not maintained as long. But the three types of treatment did not differ from each other, possibly because of the small sample size, shortness of therapy, or nonspecific treatment effects. Results should not be generalized to individual treatment, since group therapy has elements not present individually such as mutual support and shared coping strategies.

CASE EXAMPLE

Susan was a 42-year-old female. At the time of her referral for therapy, she had quit her office equipment sales job 2 months earlier and was working approximately 30 hours per week for a temporary secretarial service. She had been divorced for 3 years, after a 13-year marriage. She reported that the divorce had been relatively peaceful and that she and her ex-husband continued to communicate monthly. She described her relationship with her 15-year-old daughter as "rocky," but attributed the difficulties to normal parent–adolescent differences. Susan reported having been in short-term marital therapy, followed by divorce mediation 4 years earlier, but had never seen an individual therapist. She had been raped 10 months prior to seeking treatment, and 3 months following the assault had requested antianxiety medication from her doctor "to help her sleep." Until the past 2 weeks, she had been taking 0.5 mg of alprazolam (Xanax) per day, but reported that she wanted to stop depending on the medication.

Presenting Complaint

At her initial visit, Susan described herself as having been a "nervous wreck" since the rape. She was motorically active during the interview, her speech became increasingly pressured as she discussed her difficulties, and she was tearful during the majority of the session. She described the reason for seeking therapy as her inability to function effectively in her job and inability to feel comfortable in the presence of men. Since the assault she had become avoidant of enclosed spaces, particularly elevators and public restrooms, and of being alone with men, especially "businessmen." Although she experienced few difficulties being at home, either alone or with her daughter, she had become almost completely avoidant of public places, apart from her temporary jobs, because of the potential of being confronted with these feared situations.

History of Sexual Assault

The rape had occurred 10 months earlier. She had been asked out for a drink by a male sales client with whom she had done business for over a year. Following several drinks, he had asked her to dinner and explained that he needed to stop by his apartment on the way to check his phone messages. She accompanied him into his apartment building, and when the elevator door closed he stopped the elevator and began to knock her head against the wall and to rip off her clothes. As she struggled to open the elevator door, he pulled his tie around her neck and threatened to choke her if she did not cooperate. He took the elevator to his floor, dragged her to his apartment, and repeatedly raped her and beat her with his belt, and forced her to engage in oral sex. The assault lasted for approximately 2 hours. He eventually pushed her out into the apartment hallway where she called her sister, who picked her up and drove her to the hospital.

While at the hospital she was questioned by the police and a formal report was made. She contacted her lawyer 2 days later. After a lengthy discussion of the implications, she decided to press charges. The case had yet to come to trial when she entered treatment.

For 2 weeks following the assault, Susan did not go to work. Upon returning to work she conducted all client-related business over the phone, and made no sales calls in person. On the rare occasions that she had to meet with clients, she convinced co-workers to come with her, but after several months they refused to do so. Susan experienced decreased ability to concentrate at work. She had daily intrusive thoughts about the rape and intense physical reactions including racing heartbeat, heavy sweating, shortness of breath, and dizziness when confronted with males at work, when riding in elevators, and when alone in any confined office space.

Over the course of the next several months she came to avoid such situations completely. She described herself as "jumpy," with frequent headaches and stomachaches. After 2 months, she began to experience vivid flashbacks of the rape which further disabled her work performance. After 5 months, her boss confronted her with complaints he had received from clients regarding her availability and her decreased sales activity, and informed her that her interactions with clients must be increased. After 8 months she quit her job and began working for a temporary service. Because of the large cut in salary and less than full-time work, she reported increasing financial difficulties about which she ruminated frequently.

Soon after the rape, Susan's sleep and appetite began to deteriorate, and after 3 months she began to have recurrent nightmares related to the incident, which were still present when she began therapy and led to avoidance of sleep. She had lost 10 pounds at the time of the interview and reported no improvement in her appetite. Prior to the assault she had dated several times per month, but had not accepted the decreasing invitations since the rape. Although she believed that not all men were like the one who raped her, she was "too scared to risk finding out who was and who wasn't." Her only social activities since the rape had been with her parents and sisters, who were initially understanding but had voiced frustration over her seemingly self-damaging behavior during the past several months. At the time of the initial interview she reported little desire to spend time with old friends or to make new ones.

Assessment

Assessment consisted of a semistructured interview to obtain information related to the assault and her functioning since the assault. Several paper and pencil instruments were also administered with the following results:

Susan's score on the BDI was within the moderately depressed range. She endorsed items related to both cognitive and vegetative symptoms of depression. Susan's overall score on the Veronen-Kilpatrick Modified Fear Survey was also elevated, and she showed specific elevations on the social-interpersonal fears and rape fears subscales. Her MMPI profile showed

F-8-2 elevation indicating acute distress such as anxiety, jumpiness, inability to concentrate, and somatic problems. Fears of loss of control, distrust of others, and a history of being hurt by others were also indicated. Her score on the MMPI PTSD scale (42) was above the cutoff for identifying PTSD patients. Her scores on the Social Adjustment scale indicated distress in the areas of work and social and leisure adjustment. The information gathered suggested that Susan's symptoms met most of the DSM-III-R criteria for PTSD.

At the end of the assessment, Susan and the therapist agreed that the primary goal of therapy would be to decrease Susan's anxiety response to the rape-related stimuli (elevators, public restrooms, men, intrusive thoughts about the rape). Given the multiple nature of the feared stimuli and Susan's current high level of distress, the therapist and client determined that graded exposure accompanied by relaxation and cognitive coping strategies would be the treatment of choice. Concurrent goals for treatment also included increased social interaction, improved self-care (improved diet and exercise), and if needed, problem-solving skills training to reduce financial, job, and parenting stresses.

Treatment

The primary goal of the initial treatment session was to normalize Susan's responses to the rape and to increase her understanding of how therapy might help her to cope with its impact and reduce her symptoms. In particular, the maintenance of phobic symptoms through the continued avoidance of feared stimuli was given as a rationale for the cognitive-behavioral exposure treatment. During the first session, Susan was taught a cued progressive muscle relaxation technique and was instructed to practice once a day. Emphasis was placed on Susan's becoming aware of her feelings of tension and relaxation while using the procedure. To prevent a potential failure experience, she was asked not to begin using the technique as a coping mechanism until it was fully mastered.

During the second session, Susan reported improvement in her ability to relax, and therefore, the length of the relaxation procedure was reduced by combining muscle groups. After reviewing the physiological components of Susan's anxiety (increased heart rate, muscle tension, dizziness, difficulty breathing, sweating), the cognitive component of anxiety was introduced. The relationship between thoughts and anxiety was explained and examples given of how different interpretations of the same event can result in different affective responses.

The majority of the third session was spent having Susan identify the thoughts that were present when she experienced rape-related anxiety. Susan reported extreme thoughts such as "I don't have any control over what others do to me," "I can never trust anyone again," "If I have to be alone with a man, I will die from the anxiety," "I'll never get my life back in order," and "I am a stupid person because I put myself in the position of getting raped." To gather more information about her thoughts and to increase Susan's ability to identify thoughts, she was instructed to record any additional automatic thoughts that occurred to her during the next week.

During the next three sessions, the relaxation procedure was practiced and reduced by combining muscle groups, and Susan continued to improve her ability to identify and reduce tension. By the sixth session, Susan was instructed to use the relaxation procedure to help her fall asleep.

The majority of the sixth through ninth sessions was devoted to having Susan realistically evaluate her automatic thoughts and challenge the cognitive errors she was frequently making. When indicated, errors in Susan's thinking were modified by education (e.g., she was informed that people do not die of anxiety). Susan's all-or-none thinking regarding the trustworthiness of others and her own abilities to relate to men were challenged. Her labeling of herself as stupid and her personalization of the responsibility for the rape were modified.

It appeared that Susan did not actually lack social skills, but her beliefs that she could not interact with men or exert any control over the behavior of others toward her were decreasing her ability to interact effectively with others. Therefore, several sessions were devoted to planning and practicing strategies by which Susan could interact with others in the manner she desired. Throughout therapy Susan agreed to assignments to interact with old friends in increasingly anxiety-provoking situations. At first, Susan invited friends over for dinner, she then went to their homes, and finally began to meet them in more public places. Susan appeared to respond well to these assignments, in part due to the positive reinforcement she received from her friends, who were glad to be spending time with her again. After several weeks she was initiating such activities on her own.

Throughout treatment Susan's affect during the sessions became increasingly less labile and she appeared more relaxed. When her general level of distress appeared to have been reduced and she had become able to discuss her thoughts and feelings without discomfort, plans were made for Susan to be directly exposed to elevators, public restrooms, and being alone with a man. Four in vivo exposure-by-flooding sessions (one for each stimulus and an additional session for generalization to other men) were conducted in the therapist's office building, while Susan was using her relaxation and cognitive skills to eliminate her avoidance behaviors. These sessions typically lasted from 1½ to 2 hours, and Susan experienced intense anxiety at first, followed by reduced anxiety toward the end of the session. The therapist prevented avoidance behaviors during these sessions. Susan responded to the exposure sessions relatively rapidly and achieved generalizable results, possibly due to the cognitive exposure already achieved and her overall decreased level of distress.

By the 18th session, Susan reported a significant decrease in avoidance behaviors and intrusive thoughts and an increase in her social activities, ability to sleep, and appetite. After accepting three dates, she described feeling more confident after each one and genuinely enjoying herself once she was able to relax and handle her anxiety-provoking thoughts. One session was spent in brief problem solving to help Susan look for a new job and manage her finances and also to reinforce the progress she had already made in these areas. A final session was spent in discussing relapse prevention, especially regarding her need for continued exposure to the previously feared stimuli. Susan indicated that she felt confident in her ability to manage distressing thoughts or physiological anxiety that might periodically occur, and that she would schedule an appointment for a "booster session" in the future, if needed.

Chapter 7
Treatment of Depression

Most of the early studies on the psychological sequelae of rape reported fear and anxiety as the predominant symptoms (Burgess & Holmstrom, 1974; Notman & Nadelson, 1976; Queen's Bench Foundation, 1976; Sutherland & Scherl, 1970). However, in describing victim reactions, depressive symptoms have also been reported frequently (Katz & Mazur, 1979). Following rape, victims report feelings of guilt, shame, and worthlessness. Many have sleep disturbances, such as early morning wakening, and eating disturbances, such as loss of appetite or excessive weight gain. Although actual suicidal behavior during the first few weeks following assault is infrequent (less than 3% reported by Frank and Stewart, 1984), suicidal ideation is common (44% of the victims reported thoughts of suicide at 2 weeks postassault in our longitudinal study; Atkeson et al., 1982). In addition, the discussion of associated features of PTSD in the DSM-III-R states that "symptoms of depression . . . are common, and in some instances may be sufficiently severe to be diagnosed as a . . . Depressive Disorder" (American Psychiatric Association, 1987, p. 249).

Recently, several prospective studies have systematically assessed depressive symptoms in rape victims referred by rape crisis centers. Within the first few weeks following assault, victims show elevated scores both on self-report measures of depressive symptoms (Atkeson et al., 1982; Frank, Turner, & Duffy, 1979; Kilpatrick, 1984) and on structured interviews assessing depressive symptoms (Atkeson et al., 1982). Atkeson et al. (1982) found that 58% of victims reported moderate to severe levels of depressive symptoms at 2 weeks postassault. Similarly, Frank and Stewart (1984) reported that 56% of victims fell within the moderate to severe range of depression at 1 to 4 weeks postassault. In addition, 43% met the Research Diagnostic Criteria for major depressive disorder.

For most victims, depressive symptoms decrease significantly over the first few months following the assault, even without therapeutic intervention (Atkeson et al., 1982; Frank & Stewart, 1984; Kilpatrick, 1984). The following case is typical.

> Sally is an attractive 16-year-old. She is an only child, lives with her parents, and is reportedly close to them. Her psychological history revealed no previous depressive reactions, no previous suicidal plans or attempts, no previous psychological treatment, and no previous psychotropic medications. She did report a history of some anxiety-related illnesses, such as ulcers and headaches. Her social history indicated that prior to the assault she had two close female friends in whom she could usually confide without difficulty and that she had recently begun dating and was sexually inexperienced.
>
> She was assaulted while driving home from work in the evening. A man in a car forced her car off the road into a ditch and raped her at knifepoint. During the assault he told her that he had been following her for over a month, knew her name and where she lived, and that he would kill her if she went to the police. Following the assault Sally was able to confide in her parents, her two girlfriends, a male friend, and her school principal. Except for the two girlfriends, she described the reactions of these people as positive, supportive, and understanding. She described her girlfriends' reactions as awkward, uncomfortable, and wanting to avoid the topic.
>
> During the first 2 weeks following the assault, Sally had sleep disturbances (i.e., repeated nightmares, waking during the night, and waking early in the morning), a weight loss of over 10 pounds, and reported feeling sad and discouraged. Examination of her responses on the Beck Depression Inventory indicated a number of negative self-statements including "I feel that there are permanent changes in my appearance that make me look unattractive," "I feel I have failed more than the average person," "I am disgusted with myself," and "I am critical of myself for my weaknesses and mistakes."
>
> One month following the assault, Sally was still moderately depressed as measured by the Beck. She reported feeling blue and discouraged but kept up her activities (i.e., work) to avoid thinking about the rape. She continued to have sleep and appetite disturbances. Her preoccupation with self-blame appeared to be lessening and the number of negative self-statements that she checked on the Beck had decreased.
>
> Two months following the assault, Sally's score on the Beck was in the mildly depressed range. Her negative self-statements had continued to decrease. For example, now she checked "I am worried that I am looking old or unattractive" rather than "I feel that there are permanent changes in my appearance." She still had mild sleep disturbances, but her appetite was normal.
>
> Six months following the assault, Sally was no longer depressed. She reported feeling enthusiastic about her senior year in high school and was looking forward to college. She was doing things with her two girlfriends again and had had one date. She had entered a beauty contest, won third place, and reported feeling attractive, more independent, and confident.

By 1 year postassault, studies have shown that average victim scores on paper-and-pencil measures are not significantly different from nonvictim controls (Atkeson et al., 1982; Kilpatrick, 1984), but 25% of the victims still exhibit mild to severe levels of depressive symptoms (Atkeson et al., 1982). Victims who report more problems immediately following the assault, who have very little support from family and friends, and who have a history of poor psychological adjustment prior to the assault appear to be at greater risk for continued problems with depression. Older victims and poor victims also are at greater risk.

Other studies have assessed depressive symptomatology in victims several years postassault and found elevated scores on paper-and-pencil measures of depressive symptoms (Cohen & Roth, 1987; Ellis et al., 1981a; Santiago et al., 1985). In the study by Ellis et al. (1981a), victims were interviewed an average of 3 years postassault (range = 1 to 16 years). Most reported being depressed for some time after the assault and 50% reported having suicidal thoughts following the assault. At the time of the interview, 45% were moderately to severely depressed. Although their activity level was not impaired, victims did report obtaining significantly less enjoyment from activities. Those who were victims of sudden and violent assaults were especially likely to have persistent problems with depression (Ellis et al., 1981a). An example is the following case.

> Diane is a 29-year-old woman who works as a nursing administrator in a small private hospital. She has never been married, has no children, and is presently living alone. The assault occurred 2½ years ago at 3:00 in the morning while she was asleep in her apartment. She was awakened suddenly by a man on top of her with a knife at her throat. Immediately he said, "Don't move or I'll kill you," and made a shallow cut across her throat. The assault lasted more than 3 hours, during which she was repeatedly raped orally, anally, and vaginally. Throughout the assault the assailant continued to make shallow cuts on her arms, breasts, legs, and genitals. Interspersed among the threats of killing her and the actual physical injury were statements such as "I want you to enjoy this" and "We're going to do this until you have a good time."
>
> After the assailant left, Diane ran next door and woke up her best friend. Together they called the police and the rape crisis center. Her friend stayed with her through the police interview and trip to the hospital and for several days following the assault. On the afternoon of the assault Diane called her boyfriend of 2 years and told him about the assault. His immediate reaction was "Are you OK?" When she started to cry, he said, "I'll call you back." When she did not hear from him for several weeks she called him again and he said, "I'm sorry; I can't handle it." Diane never saw him again.
>
> For the first few weeks after the assault Diane had difficulty sleeping. She took sleeping pills to fall asleep but would awaken screaming and shaking from nightmares. She felt nauseous every time she tried to eat; she essentially stopped eating and lost 40 pounds. She repeatedly took showers, brushed her teeth, and gargled to try to wash away the odor she associated with the assailant. She was terrified to be alone and reported being afraid that she was going to start screaming and not be able to stop.
>
> During the first year and a half following the assault Diane worked compulsively with the police to catch the assailant. She felt a strong need to

find the assailant and to make him understand what he had done to her—that somehow that would make things all right again. Finally, she came to realize that this behavior and her dysfunctional thoughts about catching the assailant were only prolonging, and even exacerbating, her reaction to the assault.

In the months following the assault, Diane withdrew from most social contacts and activities. With the few close relationships that she did maintain, she became overly dependent and her friends, in turn, became overly protective. Although supportive, these relationships served to maintain her feelings of helplessness, incompetence, and inadequacy.

When Diane was interviewed 2½ years after her assault, she was severely depressed. Her score on the BDI was 37. Although she continued to function adequately in her job, she remained socially withdrawn. She had not dated since the assault and reported that she had lost all interest in sex. She still had a poor appetite and had difficulty with early morning wakening. She also reported chronic feelings of hopelessness, helplessness, sadness, and self-blame.

Sampling differences may have contributed to the contradictory findings between the studies reporting normal levels of depressive symtomatology 1 year postassault and those reporting long-term problems with depression. In the former studies victims were recruited through rape crisis centers within a few weeks of the assault and followed for 1 year. For the most part, these victim participants were young, poor, and uneducated. In studies finding long-term problems with depression, victims were recruited through media campaigns and were typically middle class. In addition, factors affecting the decision to report the assault and the unintended treatment effects of repeated assessment in the former studies may have resulted in a quicker resolution of the assault. In contrast, victims in the long-term studies were less likely to seek help immediately following the assault and may have volunteered to participate in the research because of unresolved effects of the assault.

In an attempt to overcome some of the aforementioned methodological problems, Kilpatrick, Best, Veronen et al. (1985) recently interviewed a random, representative sample of 2,004 adult women about their victimization experiences and mental health problems. Forty-four percent of the victims of completed rape reported suicidal ideation and 19.2% reported suicide attempts. Assessment of the timing of these mental health problems indicated that most occurred after the victimization. In their clinical follow-up (Kilpatrick, Veronen et al., 1987), they found that 8.6% of victims of one rape and 20% of victims of two rapes currently met the diagnosis for major depressive disorder and that 45.7% of victims of one rape and 80% of victims of two rapes met the lifetime diagnosis of major depressive disorder.

It is apparent from the aforementioned studies that a large number of victims do experience significant problems with depression immediately following sexual assault and many continue to have problems with depression years following the assault. Victims with a history of poor psychological adjustment prior to the assault and victims of violent or prolonged attacks appear at greater risk for persistent problems with depression.

INDIVIDUAL TREATMENT

Although there are several behavioral and cognitive-behavioral therapies for the treatment of depression that have been well researched, only one study has evaluated the specific treatment of depressive symptoms with sexual assault victims. Frank and Stewart (1983) adapted Beck's (1972) cognitive behavior therapy program for use with recent victims of sexual assault. Potential treatment candidates are first given a rationale for Beck's cognitive therapy:

> While many people believe that we first become depressed, anxious or fearful and then begin to think depressing or anxiety provoking thoughts, the reverse may actually be the case. That is, we come to feel depressed or anxious or fearful because we permit ourselves to have depressing or anxiety provoking thoughts. In the context of Cognitive Therapy we refer to these thoughts as "automatic thoughts." They are "automatic" inasmuch as they tend to crop up without our voluntarily willing them to come. They are "negative" inasmuch as they involve negative attributions about the self, the world, and the future. . . . we now know a good deal about the nature of such thoughts. They tend to be irrational. That is, there is little or no objective evidence to support them. They tend to be over inclusive. That is, they involve generalizing from a very small event or category of events to a large universe of events or situations. They tend to be catastrophic in nature, assuming the worst of all possible outcomes. And, most important, these thoughts cause us to experience feelings of depression, fear, and anxiety. (Frank & Stewart, 1983, p. 318)

At the first interview with a potential therapy candidate, the victim is also given a copy of *Coping with Depression* (Beck & Greenberg, 1974) to read before beginning treatment and is asked to fill out a daily activity schedule (Beck, Rush, Shaw, & Emery, 1979) for the few days before her first treatment session.

At the first treatment session, the therapist and client discuss the client's reactions to the assigned reading and review her daily activities. In the initial sessions, the daily activity schedule is used to assess how active the client actually is; many victims, when they seek treatment, have severely restricted their activities and, concomitantly, engage in self-debasing and pessimistic cognitions related to their lowered activity level. If indicated, initial treatment goals may include increasing the client's activity level, and a part of each treatment session may include using the daily activity schedule to plan activities for each hour of the day. After several sessions the client is asked to evaluate the quality of her daily activities by recording the degree of "mastery" and/or "pleasure" experienced with each activity. Again, a part of each treatment session may include planning specific activties which will give the client a sense of mastery and/or pleasure. Efforts to increase either the number of activities or the quality of activities are accomplished through graded task assignments that the client is reasonably certain to complete and, thus, experience success.

Although Beck's cognitive therapy includes these behavioral techniques to produce direct changes in the client's dysfunctional behavior patterns and associated negative estimates of her capabilities, the major emphasis of treatment involves cognitive techniques which focus directly on the cognitive components of the victim's depression. During the initial sessions in which the rationale is presented and the pamphlet *Coping with Depression* (Beck & Greenberg, 1974) is discussed, automatic thoughts or cognitions are defined and the relationship between thinking and feeling discussed and demonstrated. Because many victims have difficulty identifying dysfunctional thoughts or images and grasping the connection between thoughts and feelings, the therapist first helps the victim become aware of her own negative cognitions during the therapy session. Often the list of daily activities can be used to elicit automatic negative thoughts related to recent events over the past week. Once the victim is able to recognize the presence of her own automatic thoughts, she is asked to keep a daily record of dysfunctional thoughts. Initially, she is asked to record three things: (a) the situation or event which led to the unpleasant emotion, (b) the feeling or emotion, and (c) the automatic thought that preceded the emotion. For example, the victim might be instructed to monitor changes in her affect and to use this as a cue to recognize the dysfunctional thoughts associated with the unpleasant emotion. The victim's daily record of dysfunctional thoughts is reviewed during the therapy session and together the victim and therapist try to identify the cognitive distortions that are related to the automatic thoughts and to construct alternative, more rational, and adaptive explanations.

Two cognitive techniques suggested by Beck et al. (1979) to facilitate this process are "reattribution" and "alternative conceptualization." Because depressed persons frequently attribute or assign the blame or responsibility for adverse events to themselves, the victim is taught to review objectively the relevant events in a situation (i.e., all the extraneous factors that might have contributed to the adverse experience) and then make an appropriate reassignment or reattribution of responsibility. Depressed persons also frequently show a systematic negative bias in their interpretation of events. By helping the victim learn to generate alternative conceptualizations or interpretations, she can gain insight into her bias and counter her negative thoughts with a more accurate conclusion. Gradually, as therapy progresses, the victim is able to proceed through this process more independently and to generate her own alternative conceptualizations or reattributions for events associated with negative affect. At this point the victim is asked to record two additional things on her daily record of dysfunctional thoughts: (a) her rational response to the automatic thought, and (b) the outcome or effect the rational response had on countering the automatic thought. Beck et al. (1979) noted that many of their patients kept their daily records and reviewed them following termination of treatment as a reminder of the cognitive distortions which contributed to their depression.

Frank and Stewart (1983) adapted Beck's treatment program for individual therapy with victims of recent rape. Treatment outcome data indicate beneficial effects from their program in that treated victims show reduced depressive symptoms (Frank et al., 1988); however, their study did not include either a waiting list control or a placebo treatment control, thus confounding treatment effects with the expected improvement in victims during the first few months postassault (Kilpatrick & Calhoun, 1988). Although this treatment program has not been evaluated with depressed victims of nonrecent assault, it has been evaluated extensively with other populations and, based on these data, would be expected to be of beneficial use with depressed sexual assault victims as well.

Koss and Harvey (1987), in their chapter "The Clinical Treatment of Rape," also included a section on maladaptive cognitions and beliefs. They recommended, as part of their therapeutic strategies, careful examination of the victim's thoughts and beliefs concerning her own assault and sexual assault in general. Specific assessment of the victim's views as to the cause of her assault, the degree to which she blames herself, and even her expectations concerning the long-term impact of the assault may be beneficial to individual case conceptualization and to selection of target maladaptive cognitions.

Not all of the victim's cognitions concerning the assault are necessarily maladaptive. Some cognitions which at first glance appear maladaptive may serve to facilitate recovery. For example, Janoff-Bulman's (1979) research differentiates between two types of self-blame: characterological and behavioral. Within Janoff-Bulman's conceptual framework, characterological self-blame is a maladaptive, self-deprecating response, involves negative attributions to one's character, and is associated with depression. Examples of characterological self-blame include: "I'm too trusting, I'm a weak person, I'm too naive and gullible, I'm the kind of person that attracts trouble, I'm immature and can't take care of myself, I'm basically a bad person" (Janoff-Bulman, 1979, p. 1806). In contrast, behavioral self-blame is an adaptive, control-oriented response which focuses on one's own behavior and may help to reestablish a victim's sense of control over her life. Examples of behavioral self-blame include: "I shouldn't have let someone I didn't know into the house, I shouldn't have been out that late, I shouldn't have hitchhiked, I shouldn't have left the window open, I should have locked my car" (Janoff-Bulman, 1979, p. 1086). Janoff-Bulman (1979) suggested that cognitive therapy which includes helping victims change their attributions from characterological to behavioral might be of value in treating depressed victims. Helping victims focus on behaviors which are alterable may reduce feelings of helplessness and increase perceived control of future events. However, behavioral self-blame which might restrict a victim's daily activities and/or lifestyle should be avoided.

The beneficial effects of behavioral self-blame on subsequent recovery have received empirical support with some victim groups (e.g., spinal-cord–injured accident victims) but not with victims of sexual assault. In fact, with victims of sexual assault the more victims attributed blame to themselves (either behavioral or characterological) the more severe their postrape symptomatology (Meyer & Taylor, 1986). Behavioral self-blame may or may not serve to reduce anxiety and provide a greater sense of control over one's life, but it does not appear to be associated with positive adjustment in victims of sexual assault.

Obviously cognitions concerning causal attributions for the rape and their relationship to recovery can be complex. It may be more important to distinguish between perceived responsibility for the assault and perceived responsibility for one's recovery. Victims of sexual assault may show better adjustment if they believe they are not responsible for their assault but are responsible for dealing with the assault and its aftermath now that it has occurred (Wortman, 1983). In sum, the therapist must be able to facilitate cognitive reappraisal of maladaptive cognitions which serve to maintain depressive symptoms and dysfunctional behavior patterns while, at the same time, supporting those thoughts and beliefs which are adaptive and facilitate recovery.

GROUP TREATMENT

Several authors have argued that group therapy may be a more useful approach than individual therapy for treatment with sexual assault victims because of the beneficial effects resulting from interaction with other victims (Roth, Dye, & Lebowitz, 1988; Resick et al., 1988). To date, published reports of group treatments have had as their primary focus the anxiety and fear which follows sexual assault. However, several group treatments have monitored concomitant changes in depressive symptomatology.

Roth et al. (1988) evaluated the effectiveness of a year-long psychotherapy group with nonrecent sexual assault victims. Treatment conceptualization was based on Horowitz's (1976) model of psychological response to trauma and was designed to help the victim assimilate and resolve the trauma experience by gradually reexperiencing the trauma and its implications at manageable levels. Although not specifically developed to target depressive symptoms, depression and other psychological aftereffects were assessed initially and at several time periods during treatment and follow-up.

In the initial sessions, a rationale for the group based on Horowitz's (1976) model was given. Information concerning victim reactions to sexual assault was also provided to help normalize the group members' individual responses to the trauma of rape. Concerning the group process, Roth et al. (1988) reported:

> The group members supported each other's efforts to continue working therapeutically in the face of significant distress, and to find a better resolution or adaptation to difficulties. Working together with people of similar experiences provided a common bond which served to normalize the experience and reduce the sense of isolation and alienation that is common. The common bond allowed for the identification of common issues, the sharing of coping methods, and the attainment of insight. The group also provided its members with a sense of hope by giving them the chance to witness people arrayed along a continuum of recovery. Finally, by listening to others' stories, members often became aware of important aspects of their own trauma that had to be resolved. (p. 85)

Roth et al. (1988) emphasized that treatment was, especially in the beginning stages, a painful process and that initially there was a worsening of symptoms. Rape-related fears, intrusive thoughts, and social adjustment all showed improvement by the midpoint of the group. Depressive symptoms did not decrease significantly until the second half of the group and did not decrease to normal levels by the end of treatment. However, the treatment-related reduction in depressive symptomatology was maintained at 6 months posttreatment.

Resick et al. (1988) compared the effectiveness of three types of brief therapy in a group format with sexual assault victims. The three types of therapy were stress innoculation training, assertiveness training, and supportive psychotherapy. All groups were held for six 2-hour sessions and were co-led by a male and female therapist. At the first session all three groups were given a cognitive-behavioral explanation of the development of fear and anxiety. The remaining five sessions followed a format specifically developed for each group's treatment orientation. In the stress innoculation training group, members were taught a number of cognitive-behavioral techniques including progressive relaxation, the quieting reflex, thought stoppage, guided self-dialogue, and covert rehearsal. The assertiveness training group was based on techniques and exercises presented in Lange and Jakubowski (1976) and included both behavioral rehearsal of assertive responses and practice in changing nonassertive cognitions and faulty thinking patterns. In the supportive psychotherapy group the co-therapists served as facilitators for discussion topics selected by the group members. (A more detailed presentation of both stress innoculation training and assertiveness training can be found in chapter 6.)

Although all three groups had as their main focus the treatment of rape-related fear and anxiety, treatment effects were obtained for depression as well. Pre- to post-treatment comparisons showed significant decreases in depressive symptoms for all three groups. These treatment effects were still apparent at a 3-month follow-up but were not maintained 6 months after treatment.

In sum, the victim's immediate reactions to sexual assault include depressive symptoms—in addition to the more frequently reported symptoms of fear and anxiety. For many victims, the depressive symptomatology decreases to normal levels over the first few months following the assault. However, many victims continue to experience debilitating problems with depression years after the assault. The therapist's assessment of victims of sexual assault should always include a thorough evaluation of depression and problems related to depression (e.g., activity level, feelings of pleasure and mastery associated with activities, and negative or distorted cognitions). Equally important, the therapist's assessment of depressed women presenting for treatment should always include questions specifically designed to determine if the woman has a history of sexual assault.

In the majority of cases, victims will present with multiple problems (e.g., depression in addition to anxiety, sexual dysfunction, relationship issues). There are no clear guidelines for prioritizing treatment of target problems, for selecting treatment techniques, or for determining treatment format. Such decisions will have to be based on the results of a thorough assessment and the clinical judgment of the therapist.

CASE EXAMPLE

Becky is a college-educated 25-year-old female. At the time of her initial referral, she was unemployed, recently divorced, and living alone. She had been raped 1 year prior to seeking treatment. She described a stable family environment during childhood and a close relationship with both of her parents. After finishing college, she met her husband at the company where they both worked, and they were married shortly thereafter. Her prior psychological history revealed no previous suicidal plans or attempts, no previous psychological treatment, no previous psychotrophic medications, and no previous hospitalizations. She did report one episode of moderate depression during her senior year of college when she was taking a course overload and had some interpersonal difficulties with a friend.

Presenting Complaint

At her initial visit Becky was depressed with suicidal ideation. She reported feelings of inadequacy and helplessness. Examples of suicidal thoughts included such statements as "I'd be better off dead" and "I'll never be happy again, so what's the use of going on." Careful examination indicated no plan of action with respect to her suicidal thoughts. Becky also reported that over the past few months she had become socially withdrawn. She rarely left her apartment—maybe once a week for a short errand. She had no contact with friends and had infrequent phone contact with her parents. She stayed in bed a large part of the day and had difficulty sleeping more than a few hours each night. She also had lost 15 pounds over the last 2 months.

History of Sexual Assault

The assault had occurred 12 months prior in the apartment where she and her husband were living. Her husband was away for the evening visiting a friend. She was alone reading when the lights went out. She stepped outside her door to see if other apartments had lost their electricity. While she was standing outside, a man in workman's clothes walked up to her. He stated that he was from the power company and was there to restore the electricity. She felt uneasy and moved toward her door. Suddenly he grabbed her around the neck and forced her inside the apartment. She struggled but he choked her. He pulled her into the kitchen and obtained a knife. Threatening to kill her, he raped her at knifepoint. He then shoved her in a closet and propped the door shut with a chair. She eventually worked her way free and called the police.

Her husband returned home at the same time as the police arrived. Her husband expressed concern over her welfare and accompanied her to the hospital. However, after that night he refused to discuss the assault with her.

During the first few weeks following the assault, Becky could not bear to be alone in the apartment at night nor to be in complete darkness. She became obsessed with the thought that the lights might go out at any time. She also was fearful of small enclosed places like closets or elevators. She had repetitious flashbacks of the assault—the lights going off, the threats of murder, the feelings of choking. She was suspicious of strangers and men in general. She and her husband discontinued sexual relations completely. At work she had trouble thinking, concentrating, and completing even small tasks. She was confused and disoriented and frequently forgot what she was doing in the middle of a task. Often she would leave work in the middle of the day and began to miss work several days a week. At the end of 2 months she was fired.

Her relationship with her husband remained problematic. After several months, they resumed sexual intercourse—even though Becky had severe arousal problems and was nonorgasmic. During sexual intercourse with her husband she would see the rapist's face and become hysterical. She and her husband quarreled frequently, and her husband began staying away from home often. Finally, 10 months after the assault, he announced he was leaving her for another woman.

Assessment

Assessment included a semistructured interview to obtain information on Becky's functioning prior to the assault. She was also asked to discuss the assault and her reaction during the first few weeks after the assault. Several paper-and-pencil self-report measures were administered to obtain additional information on her current psychological functioning. The results were as follows:

1. *Derogatis Symptom Checklist (SCL-90-R):* Becky showed significant elevations on the depression subscale. The anxiety and interpersonal sensitivity subscales were also somewhat elevated.
2. *Beck Depression Inventory (BDI):* Becky scored within the severely depressed range on the BDI. Statements endorsed on the BDI included "I am sad all the time," "I feel that I have nothing to look forward to," "I feel I am a complete failure," "I feel I am being punished," "I have lost all interest in other people," and "I have to push myself very hard to do anything."
3. *Veronen-Kilpatrick Modified Fear Survey (MFS):* Becky's overall fear score was somewhat elevated. She also showed specific elevations on two subscales: social-interpersonal fears and rape fears.
4. *Profile of Mood States Scale:* Becky showed significant problems on the depression-dejection, fatigue-inertial, and vigor-activity subscales. The tension-anxiety subscale was also somewhat elevated.
5. *Impact of Event Scale:* Becky obtained higher scores on the avoidance scale than on the intrusion scale.
6. *Social Adjustment Scale–Self-Report:* Becky showed elevated scores on all subscales. Particular problem areas were responsibilities at home, her social and leisure time, dating, and her relationships with extended family.

Goals established with Becky at the end of assessment were to increase her daily activity level and the pleasure or mastery she experienced each day, to decrease her dysfunctional thoughts and the concomitant negative emotions, and to increase appropriate social interactions with family and friends.

Treatment

During the first treatment session, Becky was given a copy of *Coping with Depression* (Beck & Greenberg, 1974), and a rationale for cognitive behavioral therapy was presented. A considerable portion of the session was devoted to providing information concerning typical victim reactions to rape, to helping Becky understand the impact the assault had on her own functioning, and to exploring her own beliefs and attitudes about her assault and assault in general. At the end of the session, Becky was given a daily activity schedule (Beck et al., 1979) to fill out.

During the second treatment session, *Coping with Depression* was discussed with Becky. Examination of Becky's daily activity schedule confirmed that her activities were restricted. A large part of her day was spent either in bed or watching TV. Becky acknowledged several negative cognitions related to her lowered activity level, including feelings of incompetence and inadequacy. The therapist pointed out that for most depressed persons periods of inactivity are associated with increases in negative emotions. Together, Becky and the therapist planned several specific activities for Becky to engage in at specific times over the next few days. Activities were carefully selected so that Becky could be certain to experience some successes, and included getting dressed in the morning, eating breakfast, and cleaning some of the house. Several activities were also selected specifically to provide a pleasurable experience (e.g., eating ice cream, reading the newspaper).

The next six treatment sessions focused on increasing Becky's activity level and increasing her sense of mastery and pleasure while engaging in various activities. Gradually activities outside the home were included. Becky enrolled in an aerobics class and began visiting a nearby church.

During these sessions, the therapist also used Becky's daily activity schedule to explore negative cognitions related to recent activities. Becky quickly became adept at this process, and she began keeping a daily record of dysfunctional thoughts. Becky consistently attended to the negative aspects of a situation and, as a result, often felt inadequate and helpless.

Several sessions were spent helping Becky learn to evaluate situations objectively and generate alternate interpretations of events. Again Becky responded well to this technique and was soon able to recognize negative emotions and their associated dysfunctional thoughts and to counter these rationally.

Prior to the assault, Becky had had good social relations and several close friends. Her current social withdrawal was not judged to be reflective of deficits in social skills. However, when she did begin to interact with her old friends again, many of her interactions were problematic. Her friends were ready to resume a reciprocal relationship with Becky but were unwilling to continue to listen sympathetically to her complaints of abuse and suffering. Therefore, several sessions were used to review prosocial behaviors which facilitate and maintain friendships and to discuss differences between appropriate self-disclosure in intimate relationships and self-disclosure which is perceived as excessive whining and complaining and results from maladaptive dependency needs.

During this time Becky also expressed a desire to begin working again. She had been trained as a commercial artist and was able to find a part-time job in her field for 10 hours per week. The job also had the advantage that the hours were flexible, as long as she did work a full 10 hours each week.

Four months after Becky began therapy, it was jointly decided that her sessions be reduced to every other week. Sessions continued to center around increasing her sense of mastery and pleasure and challenging maladaptive cognitions. She began to develop several friendships with males at work and church, and some time was also devoted to rape-related issues of trust and intimacy.

Six months after beginning therapy, Becky had increased her job to 20 hours per week. She had not yet begun to date but was feeling comfortable around men and was looking forward to dating again. At this point Becky expressed a desire to stop therapy to see if she could function independently again. A joint decision was made to terminate therapy with the understanding that if problems did occur when she began dating (or if she did not begin dating in the next few months) she would recontact the therapist. Periodic phone contact over the next 6 months indicated that Becky was able to maintain her treatment gains and had continued to make progress. Two years after the assault she had had several dates and had increased her work time to 30 hours per week.

Chapter 8

Treatment of Sexual Dysfunctions

Sexual assault and child sexual abuse are probably the most underrated antecedents of sexual dysfunctions in women. They are rarely discussed in the research and treatment literature. While experts agree that anxiety is a major factor interfering with satisfactory sexual functioning, they rarely relate this anxiety to previous sexual trauma. Instead, they prefer to focus on performance anxiety, inhibitions, moral sanctions, fear of loss of control, and so on. While these forms of anxiety may account for much of sexual dysfunctioning in men, it is doubtful that they are adequate to explain the problems women have in sexual functioning. Little research has focused on the sources of sexual anxiety in women. In a study conducted to examine the effects of anxiety on women's sexual arousal, Beggs, Calhoun, and Wolchik (1987) asked women to generate personally relevant sexual anxiety scenes. Rather than the expected performance anxiety situations, many of the women spontaneously gave scenes that involved sexual coercion by a man. While the subjects in this study were not sexually dysfunctional, it helps to illustrate the widespread nature of such anxiety even among sexually functional women.

The reasons for this lack of attention to sexual trauma history are unclear. One important factor may be that sex therapists have shown little interest in how sexual dysfunctions develop. In the words of Leiblum and Pervin (1980), "For the most part, sex therapy does not concern itself with the etiology of sexual dysfunctions. In a pragmatic fashion the concern is with treatment of the problem and not with how the problem developed" (p. 379). They continued, "It is fortunate that it is possible to proceed with treatment in the absence of such understanding." (p. 380) We must question whether such treatment is as efficacious as it might be were sex therapists to place traumatic sexual experiences in proper perspective in the development of sexual dysfunctions. One must suspect that many treatment failures could be traced to the failure to deal with the traumatic sexual experience underlying the dysfunction. In light of the frequency of sexual assault and child sexual abuse in women's lives, the lack of interest in these traumas that has been shown by sex therapists and researchers is a serious disservice to women. That many sex therapists prefer not to treat known victims of sexual assault is especially unfortunate given that many therapists who are interested in treating rape victims do not have special training or experience in sex therapy. As a result, many victims with sexual dysfunction problems may go without adequate treatment.

Victims with arousal problems or low sexual desire do not always need specific treatment for sexual dysfunctions. In some cases such problems are secondary to depression or anxiety and may not require specific sex therapy; however, this is not always the case. So the question arises of when to treat or refer for treatment of sexual dysfunctions. If, after careful assessment, the sexual dysfunction is determined to be the sole or primary problem or if the sexual dysfunction remains after other problems, such as anxiety and depression, have been successfully treated, treatment targeting the sexual dysfunction should be considered. If referral to a sex therapist is necessary, an attempt should be made to find one with experience in treating rape victims.

Since most sexually assaulted women who seek treatment do not reveal the sexual assault initially, if at all, a careful assessment for history of traumatic sexual experience should be included in every case when a woman seeks treatment for sexual dysfunction. It should not be surprising to find more than one such experience in the childhood or adult history of many such women.

The fact that many sexual assault victims avoid sex, sometimes for long periods of time, complicates the clinical picture. This has no doubt contributed to an underestimation of the rates of sexual dysfunction in victims. In some cases the appearance or acknowledgment of the problem may be delayed until a woman becomes sexually active again, changes partners, or tries new activities. For example, Becker and Skinner (1984) reported a case in which after many years of satisfactory sexual functioning, a woman suddenly lost all desire for sex following an incident in which she acceded to her partner's repeated requests to try oral sex. This brought about the reexperiencing of a rape that included forced oral sex. Another important factor that may enter into sexual adjustment is sexual functioning prior to the rape. Women who have satisfactory sexual experiences seem to adjust better following a sexual assault. Becker et al. (1984) found that the sexually dysfunctional victims in their sample tended to be younger and presumably less sexually experienced at the time of their assault than sexually functional victims. They also found that sexually dysfunctional victims were significantly more likely to hold themselves at least partially responsible for their assaults. No other assault variables they studied appeared to be important in determining postrape sexual functioning. However, their sample was a mixed group of rape and incest victims. This area has been studied so little that we can make few definitive statements about the relationship of specific aspects of sexual assault to later sexual functioning. That such assault has a detrimental effect on sexual satisfaction in general has been demonstrated clearly in several studies (Feldman-Summers et al., 1979; Orlando & Koss, 1983). But these women are unlikely to seek treatment unless a specific dysfunction accompanies the reduced satisfaction. Even then, many victims live with such problems for years without seeking help.

To date, little attempt has been made to develop theoretical models for sexual dysfunctions in sexual assault victims. Becker and Skinner (1983) proposed that the development of sexual problems parallels that of assault-related fears; therefore, the same two-factor learning theory might be used to explain the development of sexual problems through classical conditioning. The sexual components of the assault can be conditioned to invoke negative reactions which then may generalize to other sexual situations, behaviors, or interactions. Avoidance behavior contributes to the continuation of these negative reactions. This two-factor theory may be limited by its exclusive focus on anxiety. Thus far, however, no other model has been proposed to explain the development of sexual dysfunctions in rape victims. Beck and Barlow (1984) presented a conceptualization of sexual dysfunctions that includes cognitive-attentional processes such as cognitive interference as important variables maintaining sexual dysfunctions, especially arousal dysfunctions. This type of conceptualization is relevant for rape victims whose negative cognitions are a common source of distress. The treatment approach suggested by Beck and Barlow, though not with rape victims in mind, is relevant: gradual (self-paced) exposure with training in cognitive control.

Barlow (1986) expanded this model of sexual dysfunction to include other elements, most of which are relevant for sexually dysfunctional victims, such as negative affect during sexual stimulation, lowered perception of control over one's own arousal, and failure to recognize or acknowledge arousal when it is present (as indicated by physiological measures). Although most of the research contributing to this model has been done with men suffering from inhibited sexual excitement, the few studies done with women are consistent. However, it is not adequate to generalize from findings on men. Neither the men nor women in these studies have been assessed for history of traumatic sexual experiences. Until the impact of such experiences is taken into account, we will never have a full understanding of how sexual dysfunctions develop or progress. As a result, the development of fully effective treatment procedures will be delayed as well.

TYPES OF DYSFUNCTION

Sexually assaulted women appear to suffer frequently from multiple sexual dysfunctions, whereas single dysfunctions are more common among nonvictims. Becker, Skinner, Abel and Treacy (1982) found twice the incidence of multiple dysfunctions among their mixed group of rape and incest victims than among nonvictims. There were also differences in the types of dysfunctions reported. While the nonassaulted women complained most often about the frequency and/or intensity of orgasm or increased boredom with sex or their sex partners, the sexual assault victims most often reported response inhibitory problems. These are problems that interfere with initial sexual responsiveness and inhibit arousal. In Becker's (1983) study, 48% of rape victims reported response-inhibiting dysfunctions. Among women who were victims of both rape and incest, the figure was even higher, over 57%. The most common specific dysfunctions reported by these women were lack of arousal, lack of desire, and fear of sex. Orgasmic problems and intromission difficulties do not appear to be more common among victims than nonvictims. An exception to this is the group of women who have been victims of both rape and incest. Becker (1983) found that women in this group were significantly more likely than victims of rape alone to experience primary nonorgasmia.

TREATMENT

In the early stages of reaction to a sexual assault, it can be helpful to inform the victim that disruptions in sexual functioning are common and to be expected. If the victim has a sexual partner, education of both the victim and her partner is recommended. An understanding, supportive partner can be helpful in preventing lasting sexual dysfunctions. It is important for the victim to feel that the pace and timing of sexual activity is under her own control, to prevent rape images from being evoked. This means that communication between the partners is important (Miller and Williams, 1984). If both partners fear rejection neither may initiate sexual activity, allowing any problems to take on added significance and perhaps interfere with the relationship generally. If needed, couples therapy can be helpful in promoting good communication skills.

Since most sexually assaulted women who seek treatment do so only after a significant delay, considerations for treatment focus on the long-term victim. To date, only Becker (1983) and colleagues have published outcome data on a treatment approach developed specifically for sexual dysfunctions in sexually assaulted and abused women. This treatment approach was designed for maximum flexibility; therefore, within the overall structure of the program each client gets an individually tailored treatment program. The length and number of sessions can vary as needed and the program can be used regardless of whether the woman has a sexual partner and regardless of sexual orientation. Either a group or individual therapy format can be used. The overall goal of treatment is to help a woman regain control over her own sexuality. In doing so she learns to restructure distorted cognitions and to be assertive in expressing her own desires and preferences in sexual interactions. Since assertiveness and positive expectations are incompatible with anxiety, she learns to view sex more positively.

The first step in treatment planning is to obtain a careful sexual problem history (Becker & Skinner, 1983, 1984), which gives a detailed understanding of current functioning and problems. It can also help women become more comfortable talking about sex and establish a common language so that therapist and client know what is meant by the terminology each uses in referring to sexual activities and problems. The sexual problem history should cover five basic areas, as outlined by Becker and Skinner (1983).

1. *Problem identification.* The client is asked to give a clear description of what she experiences when attempting to be sexual. The focus should be her behavior, feelings, and cognitions, and she should be discouraged from attempting diagnostic labels, as these are frequently misused.

2. *Onset and course of the problem.* This should include how long the client has had the problem, whether onset was sudden or gradual, as well as whether and how the problem is related to her assault. The course of the problem over time should be assessed, including changes in severity and situation specificity.

3. *Cause and maintenance of the problem.* This is aimed at understanding the client's perception of the causes of her problem and factors that contribute to it. Erroneous conceptions, especially those that could interfere with her receptiveness to treatment, should be corrected.

4. *Previous treatment and outcome.* It is important to assess previous attempts at intervention and their outcome. This should include self-help efforts. In addition, it is important to rule out organic factors and medical complications, so results of a recent medical evaluation should be reviewed.

5. *Current expectations and goals for treatment.* It is important to understand what the client wants and expects from therapy. She should set her own goals, but the therapist should make sure they are specific and realistic.

The treatment package developed by Becker (1983) and colleagues (Becker & Skinner, 1983) is structured within the framework of the P-LI-SS-IT model of Annon (1976). The letters stand for different levels of intervention, and a woman moves through the various levels depending on her individual problems and needs. At the first level (P) a woman may simply need to learn to give herself permission to engage in and enjoy certain behaviors. For example, since her rape Judy could not enjoy sexual intercourse in the male superior position because the weight of her partner was an uncomfortable reminder of her assault. However, she was reluctant to suggest other positions because of her concerns about how "normal" they were and how acceptable to her partner. Once she resolved this and permitted herself to try other positions she found them enjoyable, as did her partner.

Giving limited information (LI) is an important treatment element in many cases. Giving facts relevant to a woman's particular problem can help to normalize behavior and reactions, and to relieve anxiety associated with them. Many women and their partners lack basic information about sexual behavior and responses. They are not aware of the wide range of variability in normal sexual responsiveness. Information gathered from partners, other women, books, and so forth may make them feel that there is something wrong with their own sexual responses. Relevant information received from a therapist, from other members of a treatment group, or from appropriate readings can help a woman relabel her own responses as normal and to feel more comfortable about her sexual responses.

The third level of intervention, specific suggestion (SS), may be given by a therapist or other group members when the woman herself is not able to generate ideas for specific changes in behavior that might be helpful. The fourth level of intervention, intensive therapy (IT), is used only when problems are not resolved by working through the other three levels or are associated with serious emotional difficulties or relationship problems. It was not included in Becker's (1983) treatment study. Intervention at this level is broader and deals with problems that affect sexual functioning only indirectly. It should not often be necessary once treatment has reached this point because it is assumed that serious problems with depression, phobias, general anxiety, and so on will have been identified and dealt with prior to sex therapy in most cases.

The treatment approach described by Becker and Skinner (1983, 1984) incorporates components from a variety of other treatment programs including sensate focus exercises (Masters & Johnson, 1970), Kegel exercises (Kegel, 1952), masturbatory training (Kaplan, 1974), and others. In addition, other standard behavioral techniques are incorporated as needed. These include thought stopping (Geisinger, 1969), behavioral rehearsal (Lazarus, 1966), and systematic desensitization (Wolpe & Lazarus, 1966).

Whether an individual or group therapy format is used, each woman sets her own individualized goals. Treatment then proceeds at a flexible pace based on her own needs and progress. An important aspect of treatment is the exercises and practice assignments that the client performs at home between sessions. Her progress is discussed at each session and the assignments modified as necessary.

The format used in the treatment outcome study described by Becker (1983) and Becker and Skinner (1984) is a stepwise approach in which treatment progresses through the first three intervention levels of the P-LI-SS-IT model. In that study ten 1-hour weekly sessions were conducted in either a group or individual format. The following description of the various steps in this program will give an idea of its flexibility within the general structure. Each step can include as many sessions as necessary.

Step 1: Information and Treatment Goals

The focus of this stage is twofold. First, the woman is helped to understand both the prevalence of sexual problems and the relationship between a sexual assault and subsequent problems. Because so little is said or written about sexual dysfunctions following an assault, it is not uncommon for women to believe they are alone in experiencing such difficulties. Knowing that other victims share similar problems and understanding some of the reasons these problems develop is a great relief for many. The development of sexual problems in accordance with the two-factor social learning model is discussed in detail. This should not be an intellectual exercise, rather the woman should be encouraged to relate the model to her own individual situation. In addition, she should be encouraged to look at how avoidance and other behaviors help to maintain the problem.

In Step 1 specific treatment goals are set as well. This process will have begun during the assessment phase when the history of the sexual problems is discussed and expectations from therapy are clarified. Frequently, goals as initially stated are vague and general. An important task for the therapist is to help the woman specify her goals in concrete and realistic terms without deviating from the needs contained in her global expression of goals. To help her frame her goals, Becker and Skinner (1984) suggested asking the woman to specify what she would like to be able to do on completion of treatment that she is unable to do now. Care should be taken not to impose goals that are not acceptable to the woman. Goals should be reviewed and revised when appropriate as treatment progresses. A full discussion of goals is essential. Both the client and therapist should understand and agree on treatment goals. Hastily set goals can result in treatment delays or failure.

Step 2: Body Image

The focus of the second step is on body image. Women in our society are socialized to compare themselves with an almost impossible ideal perpetuated by movies, TV, and magazines. As a result, many women are dissatisfied with their bodies and view them as unattractive. After being attacked sexually, these problems can become exaggerated. In some cases body image may be grossly distorted. A victim who may be viewed by others as attractive sometimes sees herself as ugly, fat, or old and grows to hate her body or specific aspects of it. Negative feelings about breasts and genitals are common among assault victims. Women who viewed themselves as attractive prior to the assault sometimes blame their attractiveness for making them a target for attack. Such women may gain a lot of weight or dress unattractively in an attempt to protect themselves. These issues are openly discussed in treatment and the woman is asked to find positive aspects of her appearance. Body image exercises are given as homework assignments. A typical assignment would be to take at least 30 minutes of uninterrupted time to stand nude before a large mirror and examine the body from head to foot. The victim should focus on positive aspects of her body, noting the good features of each part.

The results of these exercises are reviewed at the following session, problems noted, and encouragement given. If necessary, further exercises of this nature may be assigned. Many women find body image exercises uncomfortable and have difficulties mastering a positive body image. Therefore, it may be necessary to continue this aspect of treatment for several sessions. The assignments can be modified and expanded to deal with individual difficulties. Becker and Skinner (1984) gave several suggestions for dealing with common problems. For example, thought stopping may be used to stop the flow of negative thoughts. Women who have difficulty finding positive aspects of their physical appearance may be encouraged to focus on positive functional abilities of the body. To overcome the common problem of failing to remember positive features, a woman may be encouraged to write them down and review them several times a day. Progress in replacing negative self-statements about the body with positive ones should be reviewed periodically after treatment progresses to other issues.

Step 3: Sensual Pleasure

Body image enhancement should evolve into a focus on sensual pleasure. This involves gaining a knowledge of how one's body provides pleasure and what is sexually arousing. Therefore, physical touching is incorporated into the body image exercises. The woman is instructed to explore her body from head to toe, including all body parts and varying the type and pressure of the touch. This will help her become aware of what is pleasurable and what is arousing for her.

Step 4: Cognitive Distraction

This step in the program is designed to deal with the common problem experienced by rape victims of cognitive distraction during sexual behavior. This cognitive distraction may result from assault-related intrusive thoughts and flashbacks or may be due to other unrelated stress and pressures. Once a pattern is established, the victim may begin to feel anxious about her ability to maintain arousal, and this in itself becomes distracting. To help control intruding thoughts, women are taught to refocus attention in ways that help maintain arousal. This should include the use of sexual fantasies, and for some women fantasy training is necessary. Homework assignments may include reading fantasy material and developing a repertoire of fantasy material that is personally relevant and arousing. Such reading material may be suggested by the therapist, although Becker and Skinner (1984) suggested that care be taken not to include fantasies involving physical force. Women should be informed that the use of sexual fantasies is normal, and any concerns or problems they have with the use of fantasies should be reviewed and discussed at each session. Since it is important to have a variety of sexual fantasies, creating and modifying one's own fantasies is included in the homework assignments. Problems may arise when modifying fantasies causes them to lose their arousal value. In this situation, Becker and Skinner found masturbatory conditioning (Abel, Barlow, & Blanchard, 1973; Davison, 1968; Thorpe, Schmidt, & Costell, 1963) an effective technique.

Step 5: Specific Sexual Dysfunctions

If specific sexual dysfunctions other than arousal problems need to be addressed, this is a good point in the program at which to begin. Standard treatment procedures from the sex therapy literature are used and will not be described in detail here. For example, women with orgasmic or arousal problems might benefit from Kegel exercises (Deutsch, 1968). Masturbatory training (Barbach, 1975; Kaplan, 1974; Lobitz & LoPiccolo, 1972) may be used for nonorgasmic women. Women with vaginismus or dyspareunia may benefit from the use of dilators (Annon, 1976; Haslam, 1965). Considerable sensitivity is needed in introducing some of these techniques since women frequently show embarrassment and have difficulty discussing their sexual functioning in such specific detail. Therapists must learn to overcome their own awkwardness or embarrassment and discuss these topics comfortably and naturally. Referral to an experienced sex therapist should be considered if these special techniques are unfamiliar.

Step 6: Physiological Responses

The physiological responses resulting in the experience of sexual arousal and orgasm are explained using visual aids when possible. In addition, women are helped to replace negative labels they have for sexual behavior or responses with more positive ones. For example, anorgasmic women who fear loss of control are helped to relabel orgasm as a positive, pleasurable experience. Such relabeling may need to take place in a stepwise fashion through the use of assignments. For example, initial assignments may involve imagining the emotional and behavioral response. This may be followed by acting out in private what an orgasm would be like. Self-stimulation exercises may be used to gain the actual experience, followed by experience with a partner if she has one. These cognitive restructuring exercises are combined with any specific sexual dysfunction exercises the woman is continuing to practice.

Step 7: Remaining Sexual Anxiety

At this stage of the treatment program, any remaining sexual anxiety is dealt with directly. If the anxiety is related to specific behaviors or situations only, alternative behaviors may be suggested. In the case of generalized anxiety, systematic desensitization may be used. Practice of these techniques is integrated into the homework assignments.

Step 8: Communication

Learning to communicate sexual needs and desires with a partner is emphasized. This includes developing assertion skills through behavioral rehearsal and, if necessary, modeling by the therapist or other group members. Role-playing with the therapist or others is helpful because problems can be identified and suggestions made. Both verbal and nonverbal components should be practiced. This training should include learning to turn down sexual overtures without fear of rejection and to redirect a partner's touches. Sensate focus exercises (Masters & Johnson, 1970) may be used to aid in sexual communication.

For women who have partners, a review of their success in communicating and especially in being assertive will be necessary. Many women have never learned to be appropriately assertive, and it is common to have difficulties in doing so. Suggestions should be made for overcoming difficulties and women should be encouraged to continue. Additional role-play may be helpful in becoming comfortable with assertiveness and finding the right words to use. It should be stressed that becoming assertive is a gradual process requiring practice and that drastic change too soon should not be expected or attempted.

Step 9: Program Assessment

Treatment goals should be reviewed and progress evaluated. Women should be encouraged to continue practicing what they have learned and not to be surprised if progress on some goals is delayed. Women without sexual partners may not be able to reach all their goals during treatment but they will have learned techniques they can apply later.

Treatment Effectiveness

Becker (1983) evaluated treatment effectiveness by having each woman rate her progress on treatment goals using a three-point scale ranging from "no progress" to "met all of the goals." At the 2-week follow-up, 81% said they had met some of the goals and 11% reported meeting all of their goals. At the 3-month follow-up, 93% reported making some progress and 6% reported meeting all goals. At 2 weeks the greatest progress was reported on goals related to rape flashbacks, increasing arousal, and self-stimulation. At the 3-month follow-up the greatest progress was on self-stimulation and dyspareunia. In comparing the group and individual treatment format, the individual format appeared to have an initial advantage soon after treatment. However, the gains made by the women in individual treatment decreased over time. Women in group treatment maintained therapeutic gains related to their sexual functioning goals. A similar pattern was seen for nonsexual treatment goals. These included general self-image, trust in others, and assertiveness. While not specific targets of treatment, improvement was seen in many of these areas and the gains were maintained better by those in group treatment. In addition, the treatment for sexual dysfunctions had a positive impact on general fear and rape-related fears. These generalized treatment gains were maintained at the 3-month follow-up session.

While these treatment outcome results are encouraging, more work must be done in this area. In particular, we need to know more about when to intervene and about what treatment techniques are most effective for which types of problems. It would be helpful if treatment outcome measures included more specific emphasis on the special problems of rape victims, such as control issues, mistrust of men, and cognitions about sexual self-esteem and self-image.

CASE EXAMPLE

Doris is a 31-year-old, middle-class homemaker. She cares for her three children, ages 2, 5, and 7, and is regularly involved in a number of church-related charitable activities. Her husband Nathan is a financial consultant for a large pharmaceutical company, and he spends an average of 8 days per month away from home. Doris dated Nathan on and off throughout high school and college and became engaged following Doris's graduation from college, when she was 22. Doris worked as a sales manager in a women's clothing store until the birth of their first child, after which she did not return to work. Doris's prior psychological history revealed a period of depression following the birth of their second child. Doris reported having seen an outpatient therapist for approximately 4 months after which her symptoms remitted. No suicidal ideation or psychotropic medication use was reported.

Presenting Complaint

Doris and Nathan attended the initial visit together. In both couples and individual interviews, they each described feeling hopeless, but were willing to make a final effort. Both Doris and Nathan reported having had an enjoyable and satisfying sexual relationship through Doris's third pregnancy. However, following the birth of their son 2½ years ago, a pattern began of Doris refusing Nathan's sexual advances. This pattern became increasingly frequent until the past 4 months, during which Nathan had ceased the advances and they had not had intercourse. During her individual session, Doris became tearful and reported that she had been raped 10 years earlier and that during the past 2 years she had been unable to stop thinking about the rape when Nathan approached her sexually. She had talked briefly with Nathan about the assault when they first became sexually active during their engagement; at that time Nathan had been understanding and patient, and within a few months they were able to have enjoyable sexual interactions.

At the completion of the initial interview, the therapist informed Doris and Nathan that, at least initially, therapy would be most beneficial if Doris came alone for the majority of sessions. This was important given the need for therapy to focus on the effects of the rape, which would probably be upsetting for Nathan and also difficult for Doris if Nathan were present. The mutually agreed-upon plan was to proceed with treatment of the rape-related difficulties, and if it was indicated Nathan might be brought into therapy occasionally. Nathan also agreed to complete several self-report instruments.

History of Sexual Assault

Doris had been raped during her senior year in college. She had been walking to her car late at night in a parking lot when a man approached her from behind, grabbed her around the neck, and held a knife to her throat. He shoved her into his car and threatened to cut her throat if she made any noise. While taunting her with insults about her body and statements such as "You are a disgusting slut," and "I hate you, you bitch" the man raped her and forced her to perform fellatio. After about 45 minutes, he yelled at her to get out of the car and he drove away. She managed to get to a phone and call her roommate. She was driven to the hospital where she was treated for knife cuts and bruises. At that time she completed a police report, but because she did not recall any identifying information other than the color of the car and the man's age and race, the police informed her that there was little chance of apprehending him. She decided not to pursue a police investigation.

Doris had told only three of her close friends about the assault before she told Natan during their engagement. Her friends had been initially supportive, but eventually became tired of her fearfulness of going places alone and of being with male strangers. For the first several weeks, Doris missed the majority of her classes, and her grades that semester were the lowest they had ever been. It was during this time that she and Nathan began dating each other exclusively and discussed the possibility of getting married. She described Nathan as the only man she had been able to trust since the rape.

After about 6 months, the rape-related intrusive thoughts and depression had decreased to the point where Doris rarely thought about the incident, and, if she did, she was able to put the thoughts out of her head. Two years prior to the assault, Doris had had a sexual relationship with a man she had dated for 1 year. She described this relationship as fun and satisfying. After the assault she reported having fears of sexual intercourse and found that she was able to put off Nathan's advances until their engagement. After an awkward sexual experience where Doris terminated the activity prematurely, she felt the need to tell Nathan about the rape. She wanted to have intercourse with him and slowly desensitized herself to being touched and became aroused enough to enjoy the interaction. After this difficult initial period, their sexual relationship became regular and spontaneous.

Assessment

Doris's complete sexual history and a thorough description of her current difficulties were obtained by means of a semistructured interview. This suggested that Doris's symptoms met the DSM-III diagnostic criteria for sexual aversion disorder. In particular, she experienced feelings of repulsion and fear to any sexual stimuli. She also reported feelings of helplessness and loss of control, similar to the feelings she had had during and after the rape. Doris had intrusive thoughts related to the rape, and often, when Nathan approached her for sex, she experienced flashbacks of the rape. On recent occasions when she had engaged in sexual activities with Nathan, she either had not become aroused or had been unable to sustain arousal, which resulted in painful intercourse and an inability to experience orgasm. Prior to the onset several years ago, she had been orgasmic 50% of the time and was satisfied with her arousal levels, suggesting a secondary pattern of dysfunction.

The general level of marital satisfaction was assessed to determine whether the sexual problem was related to any other marital problems, and whether the sexual problem could be successfully treated in the context of her marriage. Both Doris and Nathan completed the Locke-Wallace Marital Adjustment Scale (Kimmel & Van Der Veen, 1974) and received scores of 110 and 118 respectively, indicating adjustment within the normal range, but toward the lower end.

From this information and from the initial couples interview, it was determined that focusing on Doris's rape-related difficulties was an appropriate initial target, because the general level of marital distress was not likely to impede the progress of therapy and it appeared that Nathan would be a cooperative partner. No significant alcohol or drug use, evidence of personality disorders, or paraphilias were reported by either partner. Both Doris and Nathan were referred for complete medical and psychophysiological examinations, and no physiological difficulties were identified.

To assess for concurrent depression which might be maintaining the dysfunction, Doris completed the BDI and received a score of nine, indicating some mild distress but the absence of clinical depression.

From the information gained during the assessment, it was determined that Doris's difficulties could be best described as a conditioned sexual aversion with her avoidance helping to maintain the anxiety and repulsion. The high levels of stress, changes in Doris's mood, and the simultaneous interruption in their sexual activities following her third pregnancy appear to have triggered a resurgence of the conditioned response. Doris's thoughts and recognition of feelings of sexual aversion may have contributed to such an occurrence; however, a complete understanding of the origins of this relapse was not clear and was not considered necessary for treatment to proceed. Doris's difficulties with arousal, painful intercourse, and orgasm were conceptualized as resulting from the aversion and therefore were not specific treatment targets. Mutually determined goals for therapy were to decrease Doris's avoidance of sexual activity and to decrease the conditioned anxiety and feelings of repulsion. It was hypothesized that given the secondary nature of the dysfunction, reduction of these symptoms should allow for the return of her previous level of arousal and enjoyment of intercourse.

Treatment

The first treatment session was devoted to providing Doris with information concerning the etiology of her difficulties and the high frequency with which such problems occur in women who have been raped. In particular, the learned nature of her reactions to sexual stimuli and the potential for learning new responses was emphasized. To decrease the feelings of pressure and lack of control and the potential for increased anxiety, the therapist imposed a temporary ban on genital-to-genital and oral-to-genital contact. However, Doris was encouraged to touch Nathan in a nonsexual manner. At this point, Nathan was brought into the session to explain this rationale and to support and encourage him not to return Doris's touching at this point.

As homework for the next session, Doris was encouraged to focus on the positive feelings associated with touching and to write down any negative thoughts or feelings that might occur so that they could be dealt with in later sessions. In the second session, Doris reported having spent some quiet time with Nathan in which she massaged his body. She reported both positive and negative feelings: She enjoyed being physically close to him; however, she had some fear that he might touch her and that "I have no control over what he might do to me." Using this example, the relationship between her thoughts and feelings of repulsion and anxiety was explained.

Doris also identified thoughts about her body being disgusting and unattractive. To test the validity of these thoughts, she was encouraged to list five positive features of her body and with encouragement she was able to generate five relatively positive points. While doing this exercise, she stated that since the rape she had felt bad about her body and had had thoughts that her body had betrayed her by being a target for the rapist. The therapist emphasized the importance of relearning to like and appreciate all the positive aspects of her body. She was encouraged to review her five-point list each day and to add to it periodically. She was also encouraged to look at her body in the mirror and generate positive thoughts about it. As sessions proceeded, Doris became increasingly relaxed and positive when discussing her body.

During the third session, the use of masturbation as a means to become more comfortable with and to feel more in control of her body's sexual response was introduced. Although Doris had not masturbated since her relationship with Nathan began, she was comfortable doing so now, after specific plans regarding appropriate times and privacy were discussed. As a continuation of her visual exploration, she was instructed to explore her body by touching it and to notice any pleasurable or unpleasurable sensations. Possibly due to her previous success in becoming comfortable with her body, she reported no negative thoughts or feelings. During the next several sessions, Doris was encouraged to continue her self-exploration assignments and she reported continued pleasure and comfort with her body. After 3 weeks she reported experiencing orgasm during masturbation and described this as a pleasurable experience.

Doris's thoughts about her body betraying her were also discussed. Thoughts of guilt about the rape and feeling uncomfortable with experiencing pleasure during sexual interactions with Nathan were identified. Each of these thoughts was discussed and challenged, and when their irrational nature was identified and alternative views presented, Doris was able to challenge them herself.

At this point, a rationale for desensitizing Doris to Nathan's touching was presented first to her and then to Nathan. Initially, only nonsexual touching was prescribed. To increase her sense of control, Doris was instructed to ask Nathan to touch a part of her body and then after several minutes to ask him to stop. Gradually she was to increase the areas that she allowed him to touch and she was then to tell him how it felt. Using this procedure, Doris was able to tolerate and eventually enjoy Nathan's touch. Whenever she felt anxiety, she was to ask Nathan to stop, and to recall the feelings she had when she touched herself. If intrusive thoughts occurred, she was to challenge them, to use a thought-stopping procedure, or to replace the negative thoughts with positive thoughts about her body. She was also encouraged to develop a repertoire of sexual fantasies as a means of preventing intrusive thoughts. Generating sexual fantasies during sessions and encouraging her to modify these was also helpful. As Doris became able to tolerate being touched, Nathan was instructed to touch Doris but first to tell her where he was going to touch her. Role-plays of telling Nathan how she was feeling and what she enjoyed were conducted, followed by encouragement for such behaviors.

After the next session, this two-stage procedure was repeated during home assignments, first with Doris asking for the touching to start and stop, and then with Nathan telling her when he was going to touch her. During the therapy sessions the control which Doris was developing over her own body and over her interactions with Nathan was emphasized. As she began to experience feelings of sexual arousal in her interactions with Nathan, it appeared that she was beginning to mislabel these sensations as anxiety, which triggered thoughts of the rape. Therefore, the physiological feelings associated with sexual arousal were discussed and feelings of arousal were relabeled. She was encouraged to focus on the pleasurable feelings in her body, to use her sexual fantasies should intrusive thoughts occur, and to challenge thoughts about not being in control.

Given that the focus throughout treatment was on Doris's sexual activities, enjoyment, and thoughts, an important aspect of treatment was for both Doris and the therapist to support and reinforce Nathan's role in therapy. Without his cooperation therapy would have proceeded slowly at best. Fortunately, Nathan was willing to participate in the program as it was implemented, and this facilitated therapy.

After 3 weeks of sexual touching, Doris stated that she wanted to have intercourse with Nathan. The intercourse ban was lifted and some instruction was given (i.e., gradual exposure, use of cognitive strategies, Doris's exercising some control over the interaction and communicating her feelings to Nathan). Doris came in the following week describing positive feelings about the experience, and she reported having become aroused. She reported success using both cognitive strategies to cope with irrational thoughts and thought stopping to terminate a brief flashback. These positive feelings were maintained over several sessions with no major setbacks. At the final session, she reported experiencing even less anxiety during intercourse and experiencing orgasm on two occasions during the week.

The focus of the last session was on the maintenance of gains and prevention of relapse. Each of the treatment components was reviewed and the need for continued awareness of her own thoughts and feelings was stressed. Doris was encouraged to use the self-controlled procedures she had learned should further problems arise. The possibility of a relapse was considered remote, but was not ruled out, especially if negative sexual experiences or traumas occurred. Doris was told she could return for further sessions if necessary.

Chapter 9

Special Issues

This chapter addresses special issues in the treatment of sexual assault victims. While the topics are important, they have not been well researched to date. However, research is increasing at a rapid rate, as the impact of sexual assault and the importance of addressing it in therapy are recognized. Mental health professionals are urged to attend to developments in the literature regarding the treatment of rape reactions so that their knowledge base will remain current.

THERAPIST GENDER

Raped women usually seek a female therapist because they feel more comfortable talking to another woman and they may have rape-engendered distrust of men. However, a female therapist is not always available and/or a victim may not be assertive enough to request one specifically. Does therapist gender make a difference? Can male therapists work effectively with female victims? This is a controversial issue, with strong feminists frequently taking the position that men should never attempt to treat female victims because they may fail to understand the victim's reactions and be more prone to victim blaming. Although little research has been done regarding this issue, two studies have examined, in a limited way, the attitudes and behavior of male therapists toward sexually assaulted women.

Dye and Roth (1990) surveyed male and female therapists regarding their attitudes, knowledge, and treatment approaches with sexually assaulted clients. They found that female therapists were more knowledgeable about signs and symptoms that rape trauma might be the source of a client's problems. Male therapists had less positive attitudes toward victims and were more likely to accept rape myths. Therapists, regardless

111

of gender, who held more biased attitudes toward victims were more likely to endorse treatment themes and employ treatment strategies that blamed the victim. Biased and unbiased therapists were equally likely to focus on rape as an issue in treatment, leading the authors to express concern that the biased therapists might focus on aspects that are unhelpful, such as the victim's role in the assault, rather than her traumatic reactions. Other interesting findings from this study were that younger therapists and therapists trained as psychologists or social workers had more positive attitudes toward rape victims than older therapists and psychiatrists. The authors recommended that female rape victims, in the absence of specific information about potential therapists' attitudes, knowledge, and experience, seek treatment from young female psychologists or social workers who have had previous experience with or training in working with victims.

Female therapists can hold biased attitudes or be insensitive to victims' needs. Experience with such a therapist might be more harmful to a victim, because unexpected, than a negative experience with a male therapist. The most important consideration is not gender, per se, but knowledge, sensitivity, and an accepting attitude.

Silverman (1977) identified several potential problems when men work with female victims in therapy or counseling. One was the therapist's possible anxiety that he might be rejected by a client simply on the basis of his gender. Silverman proposed this anxiety as the probable basis for certain modifications in technique reported by male psychiatric residents working a rape crisis program. They spoke more softly than usual; changed their use of space, some sitting more closely than usual, others farther away; and changed their use of physical contact, some patting a hand or shoulder, others seeing this as inappropriate.

Silverman saw that perhaps the most common error made by male therapists is a tendency to focus more on the sexual aspects of the rape than on the violence, which can cause a victim to perceive the therapist as less understanding and supportive. A desire to be viewed as liberal or unchauvinistic was seen as posing another potential danger if it leads to being ingratiating or patronizing. Other dangers Silverman identified were (a) difficulty in empathizing with a female victim, which could lead to questioning her credibility or responsibility for the rape; (b) identifying with the victim's husband, boyfriend, or father, which may communicate indignation at the harm he has suffered, or overprotectiveness, confirming the victim's feelings of helplessness and vulnerability; and (c) the therapist allowing his own anxiety to interfer with dealing directly with the victim's affect, confirming her suspicion that her experience is too horrifying to discuss.

Silverman's advice to male therapists is equally appropriate for both genders—to become educated about prevalent misconceptions regarding rape; to examine personal biases, values, and beliefs that might interfere with the communication of empathy; to be aware of the reasons for a victim's diminished capacity to trust and to establish new relationships; to be aware continuously of one's own feelings and their effect on the victim; and to beware of pitfalls such as the therapists own fears of rejection or fantasies of rescuing the victim.

MARITAL RAPE

In the past, rape has been mistakenly viewed as a crime typically perpetrated by strangers. Recent research, however, indicates that women are more frequently assaulted by someone well known to them and that rape in marriage is a significant problem. Through a random community survey, Russell (1982) found that 14% of the married women in his sample had been the victim of at least one attempted or completed rape by a husband or ex-husband. Although the majority of these women also experienced other types of violence in their marriage and could best be described as battered women, for 23% of the women sexual assault was either the major or only form of violence in their marriages. Clinical observations by Finkelhor and Yllo (1982) also support the finding that marital rape is not the exclusive problem of battered women.

Another misconception in the area of marital rape is that rape by a husband is somehow less traumatic than rape by a stranger. However, rape victims are equally likely to be physically injured if assaulted by their husbands or a stranger. And victims of marital rape, when compared with victims of stranger rape, perceive the situation as equally dangerous and exhibit similar levels of fear that they might be seriously injured or killed (Kilpatrick, Best, Saunders, & Veronen, 1987). The long-term psychological consequences of marital rape are also similar to those of stranger rape. The impact of rape on a woman's overall functioning can be severe whether assaulted by a stranger or a husband. Victims of marital rape are just as likely to be depressed, fearful, or sexually dysfunctional years after their assault as victims of stranger rape (Kilpatrick, Best et al., 1987).

Because victims of marital rape exhibit many of the same psychological problems as other sexual assault victims, the treatment strategies presented in this book are applicable to this population. However, the victim's relationship to the perpetrator introduces additional issues and problems that must be carefully considered in any clinical intervention (Weingourt, 1985). Few victims of marital rape voluntarily seek treatment while in the abusive relationship. If physical battering is a factor, treatment must be provided for the batterer as well as the victim, though few batterers are motivated. Clinicians are encouraged to work with community outreach programs, shelters, and so on to improve services for their clients.

MALE VICTIMS

Although we have used examples of female rape victims only, it should be remembered that males are victimized by sexual assault as well. Unfortunately, little research has been done to document the prevalence of this problem outside of prisons, and knowledge of men's adjustment is based primarily on a few case studies and small samples. Men's reluctance to report rape has contributed to assumptions that it is rare. Most studies have used only men who reported a sexual assault. Forman (1982) found that only 5.7% of reported rapes involved male victims. Kaufman, Divasto, Jackson, Voorhees, and Christy (1980) found that 10% of rape victims during a 3-month period in 1978 were male. By comparison, 14% of male prisoners in a medium-security prison were found to have been sexually assaulted (Wooden & Parker, 1982). Burnam et al. (1988), in a large, well-controlled community survey, found that 18% of 432 sexual assault victims in the Los Angeles area were men. However, this included those assaulted as children. No separate statistics were given for those assaulted as adults.

Evidence relating to psychological reactions of male victims indicates that the impact of rape is similar in many ways to female victims. For example, Goyer and Eddleman (1984) identified posttraumatic stress symptoms in 13 male sexual assault victims who sought treatment at a Naval psychiatric outpatient center. Predominant symptoms were fear, generalized anxiety, depression, suicidal ideation, sleep disturbances, nightmares, anger, and sexual dysfunctions. In addition, however, male victims frequently worry about the implications of having been raped by another man (men are almost always the assailants) for their sexual identity or that others may view a rape as predisposing them to homosexuality. If the male offender attempts to cause the victim to ejaculate, as half did in a study by Groth and Burgess (1980), they are even more confused and distressed, and they are less likely to report the crime.

Male victims react badly to the loss of control and sense of helplessness experienced during sexual assault. They may tend to withdraw, deny the experience, avoid reminders of it, or even become amnesic. Kaszniak, Nussbaum, Berren, and Santiago (1988) reported such a case. This male victim was hospitalized with functional retrograde amnesia for all autobiographical information shortly after being raped at gunpoint by two men. He regained his memory under hypnosis and, following treatment and referral to a rape crisis center, regained much of his functional ability. However, 15 months later, he remained mildly depressed, emotionally labile, and overindulged in alcohol compared to his prerape level. That male victims may be especially at risk for substance abuse was supported by Burnam et al. (1988), who found that men who were sexually assaulted as children or adults were more likely than assaulted women to develop alcohol abuse or dependence. Gender did not predict likelihood of developing any other disorder.

It has been suggested that sexual assaults on men are more likely to involve physical brutality and multiple assailants (Kaufman et al., 1980). This is contradicted, however, by a large-scale epidemiological study (Sorenson, Stein, Siegel, Golding, & Burnam, 1987) which indicated that women are more likely to be harmed physically or threatened with harm than men. The apparent contradiction may result from the fact that a number of victims in the Kaufman et al. study were seen for treatment of physical injuries initially, with the sexual assault being revealed later.

Male victims are less likely to disclose a sexual assault to others and may not profit as much as women from social support (Gerrol & Resick, 1988), probably because of their socialization emphasizing self-reliance. For this reason, it is important that therapists be sensitive to cues that may indicate a history of sexual assault. It is likely that male victims seek treatment, if at all, for problems related only indirectly to the assault, and may never disclose it unless the therapist has the intuition to detect it. We have found the following to be a useful guide when working with either gender: Whenever a client shows the usual reactions seen in rape victims without relating an adequate precipitating event, or when a client fails to respond to treatment that would normally be effective with the presenting problem, a traumatic sexual experience should be considered. If a prior assault is discovered in a man, the treatment approaches described for use with female victims should be tried, with appropriate modifications if necessary. Almost nothing has been published on treatment of male sexual victims, but experience with male victims of other traumas (e.g., combat, accidents) appears to support the efficacy of such approaches.

ELDERLY VICTIMS

The sexual assault of older women has received little attention in the rape literature. As a result, there is a paucity of information on the incidence and characteristics of sexual victimization of the elderly and of the resulting psychological effects. Even though rape is one of the most underreported crimes, the rate of underreporting for this special population may be even higher. Estimates of the yearly incidence rate of rapes against women over 50 vary from 2 per 1,000 to 35 per 1,000 population. The prevalence of elderly sexual assault victims in the population is also difficult to estimate and probably higher than one would expect.

Although the pattern of reactions to sexual assault experienced by the elderly victim is probably similar to that of younger victims, differences should also be expected. Elderly victims may be more likely to endorse traditional beliefs and misconceptions concerning rape and, as a result, may have more difficulty with maladaptive cognitions in general. Because of their age and decreased physical capacity, the assault may exacerbate the older victim's already strong feelings of helplessness and fears of vulnerability. Financial constraints may also severely limit the older victim's ability to make changes in her environment and adequately meet her safety needs. An older victim may already be somewhat isolated and lack a readily available social network. On a more positive note, the social network of the elderly victim may be more outraged by the victimization of an older person, less likely to view the victim as somehow responsible for the assault, and more likely to provide needed support.

Because elderly victims may be less likely to disclose their victimization to others, professionals who provide services to older women need to be sensitive to changes in their overall functioning and cues that might indicate a history of sexual assault. As with any victim, treatment of the elderly victim will need to be individualized and modified to meet her specific issues and needs.

ANGRY VICTIMS

How emotions are experienced and expressed by sexual assault victims depends on the individual. This is true of anger. Outward expressions of anger can range from none at all to episodes of rage. Dealing with the angry victim can present significant challenges, especially if the anger is directed toward the therapist or seems to interfere with the progress of treatment. Behavior commonly interpreted as resistance (e.g., missed sessions, uncooperative or demanding behavior) may reflect a victim's attempts to avoid confronting her own strong, even overwhelming feelings. Anger is troubling to victims for several reasons. First, most women are socialized in ways that do not teach them to deal effectively with anger. They are taught to avoid expressing it as well as to avoid becoming the target of it. The implicit message is clear—anger is powerful and dangerous. Second, anger may be a potent reminder of the assault for some women, bringing back their own feeling at the time or those they attributed to the rapist. Women's descriptions of assailants frequently include behavior they interpret as indicating anger or rape. For example, "He threatened me in a very angry tone of voice." "He became enraged when I tried to resist." "He suddenly turned into an animal. I was terrified." Thus, becoming the target of anyone's anger can be a frightening thought that contributes to the isolation, social avoidance, and lack of assertiveness of some victims.

A third reason anger may be troubling to victims is that they rarely have an opportunity to express it directly to the assailant because he is rarely caught. Even when the assailant is known to the victim, she may be too frightened of retaliation to show her anger. Rapists often threaten to return and kill their victim if she takes any action or reports the rape. It is not surprising that many victims do not like to admit their anger, or turn it toward safer targets—the therapist, themselves, or the failure of the system to provide them justice.

Roth and Lebowitz (1988) discussed another feature of anger—that it is a motivating affect. When the behavioral expression of this motivation is blocked, a woman may be left more aware of the helplessness of her situation. Such enforced helplessness may further contribute to her sense of rage. Roth and Lebowitz also saw self-blame as possibly related to guilt over anger. Thus, the victim may see the safest route as inhibiting her anger altogether. The therapist must be aware of these possible dynamics so that careful thought can be given to the timing and method by which a victim is assisted in coping with anger.

Angry outbursts and explosive rages are perhaps most likely to be shown by those victims suffering from PTSD, in which case the treatment should be part of the total treatment approach aimed at PTSD (see chapter 5). Kilpatrick and Amick (1985) described the treatment of a rape victim who had intense anger and vengeful fantasies toward her assailants. These were conceptualized as intrusive thoughts and treated similarly to intrusive cognitions of any nature, rather than through discussion of the anger as an emotional reaction per se. She was taught coping strategies such as thought stopping and to substitute imagining or engaging in incompatible pleasant activities. This significantly reduced her intrusive vengeful thoughts. Victims may also be encouraged to refocus thoughts on positive coping they have done or to refocus the energy in angry thoughts to more constructive channels. For example, many victims find volunteer work aimed at helping other rape victims or aimed at rape prevention a useful way to channel anger and avoid feeling helpless.

PARTNER REACTIONS TO RAPE

As might be expected, rape has an enormous effect on the victim's husband or boyfriend. Not only must the partner cope with the victim's psychological distress and emotional needs, but he must also deal with his own reactions to the assault. Although reactions are variable, descriptive studies have found partners to exhibit shock, rage, self-blame, concern for the victim, and emotional distress immediately following sexual assault (Holmstrom & Burgess, 1979). Longitudinal studies of partner reactions indicate that the psychological distress (e.g., fear, anxiety, and depression) experienced by partners may be long term in nature and last for at least 1 year following sexual assault (Veronen, Saunders, & Resnick, 1988).

Such emotional distress in both the victim and her partner can also have a profound effect on their relationship. Although both the victim and her partner may need emotional support following sexual assault, each may be unable to provide sufficient support for the other because of their own distress and conflicted feelings. Victims and their partners have difficulty discussing the assault and the resulting emotions; most couples avoid the topic and have minimal or no discussions concerning the rape and its impact.

Sexual relations are frequently problematic. Following rape, many women find sexual contact aversive and may experience flashbacks of the assault when approached sexually. Intercourse is frequently uncomfortable or painful, and there may be problems with arousal and satisfaction. Partners may or may not be sensitive to the victim's feelings about sexual relations. Most partners also experience conflicted feelings about resuming sexual relations and have difficulty balancing their own needs to resume sexual relations with those of the victim.

As is apparent from the foregoing, partners of victims of sexual assault frequently need the services of mental health professionals. Treatment to address the emotional distress and maladaptive cognitions experienced by partners can be provided individually, in conjoint therapy with the victim, or through partner support groups. Helping the victim and her partner to discuss the rape and its impact on each and on their relationship is probably best accomplished in joint sessions.

CONCLUSION

Despite almost 3 decades of clinical observation and empirical research, we are only now beginning to understand the serious consequences that sexual assault can have for a woman and those close to her. A victim's cognitive, emotional, and social functioning may be adversely affected for months and even years. Whether aware of the assault or not, family, friends, and co-workers are also affected. When prevalence rates are considered, the cost to society is extensive.

Although some victims are able to use their preexisting strengths and support networks to assimilate the assault and resume prerape functioning, many need mental health services to resolve the trauma of rape and its aftermath. Despite the devastating effects of assault, most victims are reluctant to seek professional help immediately following the assault and may wait several years before they are finally seen by a clinician. When they do seek treatment, many victims—for a variety of reasons—do not reveal their assault history. Because of the high prevalence of rape in our society, it is imperative that therapists recognize presenting symptoms known to be rape induced, seriously consider the possibility of a past sexual assault, and assess for such in a sensitive and supportive manner.

Development of treatment approaches for sexual assault victims is still at an early stage. More research is needed to delineate the most effective methods. More research is also needed to fill the gaps in our knowledge about the short- and long-term effects of sexual assault and the person-situation-environment interactions that determine them. In addition, we need better and more complete theories to help us understand these effects. Finally, the field is in desperate need of prevention methods. Treatment, necessary and valuable as it is, is no substitute for prevention—prevention of sexual assault from occurring and prevention of the long-term traumatic effects that take such a toll on victims' lives.

Most of the treatment approaches we have described have demonstrated effectiveness through at least minimal outcome research. Methods should continue to evolve as we learn more about rape and its effects. We hope to see increased interest in the problems faced by victims. Study of this area has increased our understanding of victims of other crimes, natural disasters, and so on and how to help them as well. As more mental health professionals, rape crisis workers, and the public at large become aware of the availability of treatment programs for some of the most devastating consequences to victims, victims will realize they do not have to suffer alone or risk being blamed when they seek help. They have a right to demand more and better care than they have sometimes received. By getting such care at an earlier stage in the development of problems, it may be possible to prevent some of the worst effects.

References

Abel, G. G., Barlow, D. H., & Blanchard, E. B. (1973, December). *Developing heterosexual arousal by altering masturbatory fantasies: A controlled study.* Paper presented at the meeting of the Association for Advancement of Behavior Therapy, Miami, FL.

Ageton, S. (1983). *Sexual assault among adolescents.* Lexington, MA: D.C. Heath.

American Psychiatric Association. (1980). *Diagnostic and statistical manual of mental disorders* (3rd ed.). Washington, DC: Author.

American Psychiatric Association. (1987). *Diagnostic and statistical manual of mental disorders* (3rd ed., rev.). Washington, DC: Author.

Amick, A., & Calhoun, K. S. (1987). Resistance to sexual aggression: Personality, attitudinal and situational factors. *Archive of Sexual Behavior, 16,* 153–163.

Annon, J. S. (1976). *Behavioral treatment of sexual problem: Brief therapy.* Hagerstown, MD: Harper & Row.

Atkeson, B. M., Calhoun, K. S., Resick, P. A., & Ellis, E. M. (1982). Victims of rape: Repeated assessment of depressive symptoms. *Journal of Consulting and Clinical Psychology, 50,* 96–102.

Barbach, L. G. (1975). *For yourself: The fulfillment of female sexuality.* Garden City, NY: Doubleday & Co.

Barlow, D. H. (1986). Causes of sexual dysfunction: The role of anxiety and cognitive interference. *Journal of Consulting and Clinical Psychology, 54,* 140–148.

Barlow, D. H. (1988). *Anxiety and its disorders.* New York: Guilford Publications.

Bart, P. (1975, May). *Unalienating abortion, demystifying depression, and restoring rape victims.* Paper presented at the meeting of the American Psychiatric Association, Anaheim, CA.

Beck, A. T., Ward, C. H., Mendelson, M., Mock, J., & Erbaugh, J. (1961). An inventory for measuring depression. *Archives of General Psychiatry, 4,* 561–571.

Beck, A. T. (1972). *Depression: Causes and treatment.* Philadelphia: University of Pennsylvania Press.

Beck, A. T., & Greenberg, R. L. (1974). *Coping with depression.* New York: Institute for Rational Living.

Beck, A. T., Rush, A. J., Shaw, B. F., & Emery, G. (1979). *Cognitive therapy of depression.* New York: Guilford Publications.

Beck, J. G., & Barlow, D. H. (1984). Current conceptualization of sexual dysfunction: A review and an alternative perspective. *Clinical Psychology Review, 4,* 363–378.

Becker, J., & Abel, G. G. (1981). Behavioral treatment of victims of sexual assault.

121

In S. M. Turner, K. S. Calhoun, & H. E. Adams (Eds.), *Handbook of clinical behavior therapy* (pp. 347–379) New York: John Wiley & Sons.

Becker, J. V. (1983). *Sexual dysfunctions in rape victims.* Final report, National Institute of Mental Health. Grant No. MH32982

Becker, J. V., & Skinner, L. J. (1983). Assessment and treatment of rape-related sexual dysfunctions. *The Clinical Psychologist, 36,* 102–105.

Becker, J. V., & Skinner, L. J. (1984). Behavioral treatment of sexual dysfunctions in sexual assault survivors. In I. R. Stuart & J. G. Greer (Eds.), *Victims of sexual aggression* (pp. 211–233). New York: Van Nostrand Reinhold.

Becker, J. V., Skinner, L. J., Abel, G. G., Axelrod, R., & Chichon, J. (1984). Sexual problems of sexual assault survivors. *Women and Health, 9,* 5–20.

Becker, J. V., Skinner, L. J., Abel, G. G., Howell, J., & Bruce, K. (1982). The effects of sexual assault on rape and attempted rape victims. *Victimology, 7,* 106–113.

Becker, J. V., Skinner, L. J., Abel, G. G., & Treacy, E. C. (1982). Incidence and types of sexual dysfunctions in rape and incest victims. *Journal of Sex and Marital Therapy, 8,* 65–74.

Beggs, V. E., Calhoun, K. S., & Wolchik, S. A. (1987). Sexual anxiety and female sexual arousal: A comparison of arousal during sexual anxiety stimuli and sexual pleasure stimuli. *Archives of Sexual Behavior, 16,* 311–319.

Bennetts, L. (1978, April 14). The type of attack affects rape victims speed of recovery, study shows. *New York Times,* p. A16.

Blanchard, E. B., & Abel, G. G. (1976). An experimental case study of the biofeedback treatment of a rape induced psychophysiological cardiovascular disorder. *Behavior Therapy, 7,* 113–119.

Blanchard, E. B., Kolb, L. C., Gerardi, R., Ryan, P., & Pallmayer, T. P. (1986). Cardiac response to relevant stimuli as an adjunctive tool for diagnosing post-traumatic stress disorder in combat veterans. *Behavior Therapy, 17,* 592–606.

Bown, O.H., & Richek, H. G. (1967). The Bown Self-Report Inventory (SRI): A quick screening instrument for mental health professionals. *Comprehensive Psychiatry, 8,* 45–52.

Brom, D., Kleber, R. J., & Defares, P. B. (1989). Brief psychotherapy for post-traumatic stress disorders. *Journal of Consulting and Clinical Psychology, 57,* 607–612.

Burgess, A. W., & Holmstrom, L. L. (1974). Rape trauma syndrome. *American Journal of Psychiatry, 131,* 981–986.

Burgess, A. W., & Holmstrom, L. L. (1978). Recovery from rape and prior life stress. *Research in Nursing and Health, 1,* 165–174.

Burgess, A. W., & Holmstrom, L. L. (1979a). Adaptive strategies and recovery from rape. *American Journal of Psychiatry, 136,* 1278–1289.

Burgess, A. W., & Holmstrom, L. L. (1979b). *Rape: Crisis and recovery.* Bowie, MD: Robert J. Brady.

Burgess, A. W., & Holmstrom, L. L. (1979c). Rape: Sexual disruption and recovery. *American Journal of Orthopsychiatry, 49,* 648–657.

Burnam, M. A., Stein, J. A., Golding, J. M., Siegel, J. M., Sorenson, S. B., Forsythe, A. B., & Telles, C. A. (1988). Sexual assault and mental disorders in a community population. *Journal of Consulting and Clinical Psychology, 56,* 843–850.

Burt, M. R., & Katz, B. L. (1987). Dimensions of recovery of rape: Focus on growth outcomes. *Journal of Interpersonal Violence, 2,* 57–81.

Burt, M. R., & Katz, B. L. (1988). Coping strategies and recovery from rape. *Annals of the New York Academy of Sciences, 528,* 345–358.

Butcher, J. N., & Maudal, G. R. (1976). Crisis intervention. In I. B. Weiner (Ed.), *Clinical methods in psychology* (pp. 591–648). New York: John Wiley & Sons.

Calhoun, K. S., Atkeson, B.M., & Resick, P. A. (1982). A longitudinal examination of fear reactions in victims of rape. *Journal of Counseling Psychology, 29,* 655–661.

Carmen, E. H., Rieker, P. P., & Mills, T. (1984). Victims of violence and psychiatric illness. *American Journal of Psychiatry, 141,* 378–383.

Cautela, J. R. (1968). Behavior therapy and the need for behavioral assessment. *Psychotherapy, 5,* 175–179.

Chemtob, C., Roitblat, H. C., Hamada, R. S., Carlson, J. G., & Twentyman, C. T. (1988). A cognitive action theory of post-traumatic stress disorder. *Journal of Anxiety Disorders, 2,* 253–275.

Cohen, L. J., & Roth, S. (1987). The psychological aftermath of rape: Long-term effects and individual differences in recovery. *Journal of Social and Clinical Psychology, 5,* 525–534.

Coons, P. M., & Milstein, V. (1984). Rape and post-traumatic stress in multiple personality. *Psychological Reports, 55,* 839–845.

Davidson, J., Swartz, M., Storck, M., Krishnan, R. R., & Hammett, E. (1985). A diagnostic and family study of posttraumatic stress disorder. *American Journal of Psychiatry, 142,* 90–93.

Davison, G. C. (1968). Elimination of a sadistic fantasy by client-controlled counter-conditioning. *Journal of Abnormal Psychology, 73,* 84–90.

Derogatis, L. R. (1977). *SCL-90-R Manual.* Baltimore: Clinical Psychometrics Research Unit, Johns Hopkins University.

Derogatis, L. R., & Melisoratos, N. (1979). The DSFI: A multidimensional measure of sexual functioning. *Journal of Sex and Marital Therapy, 5,* 244–281.

Deutsch, R. M. (1968). *The key to feminine response in marriage.* New York: Random House.

DiNardo, P. A., Barlow, D. H., Cerney, J., Vermilyea, B. B., Vermilyea, J. A., Himadi, W., & Waddell, M. (1985). Anxiety Disorders Interview Schedule— Revised (ADIS-R). Albany, NY: Phobia and Anxiety Disorders Clinic, State University of New York at Albany.

Dye, E., & Roth, S. (1990). Psychotherapists' knowledge about and attitudes toward sexual assault victim clients. *Psychology of Women Quarterly, 14,* 191–212.

Egendorf, A., Kadershin, C., Laufer, R. S., Rothbart, G., & Sloan, L. (1981). Legacies of Vietnam: Comparative adjustment of veterans and their peers. (Publication No. V101 134P-630). Washington, DC: U. S. Government Printing Office.

Ellis, E. M., Atkeson, B. M., & Calhoun, K. S. (1981a). An assessment of long-term reaction to rape. *Journal of Abnormal Psychology, 90,* 263–266.

Ellis, E. M., Atkeson, B. M., & Calhoun, K. S. (1981b). Sexual dysfunction in victims of rape. *Women and Health, 5,* 39–47.

Feldman-Summers, S., Gordon, P. E., & Meagher, J. R. (1979). The impact of rape on sexual satisfaction. *Journal of Abnormal Psychology, 88,* 101–105.

Finkelhor, D., & Yllo, K. (1982). Forced sex in marriage: A preliminary research report. *Crime and Delinquency, 28,* 459–478.

Fitts, W. H. (1965). *Manual: Tennessee Self-Concept Scale.* Nashville, TN: Counselor Recordings and Tests.

Foa, E. B., & Kozak, M. J. (1986). Emotional processing of fear: Exposure to corrective information. *Psychological Bulletin, 99,* 20–35.

Foa, E. B., Steketee, G., & Olasov-Rothbaum, B. (1989). Behavioral/cognitive conceptualizations of post-traumatic stress disorder. *Behavior Therapy, 20,* 155–176.

Forman, B. (1980). Psychotherapy with rape victims. *Psychotherapy: Theory, Research, and Practice, 17,* 304–311.

Forman B. D. (1982). Reported male rape. *Victimology, 7,* 235–236.

Foy, D. W., Resnick, H. S., Sipprelle, R. C. & Carroll, E. M. (1987). Premilitary, military and postmilitary factors in the development of combat-related posttraumatic stress disorder. *The Behavior Therapist, 10,* 3–10.

Foy, D. W., Sipprelle, R. C., Rueger, D. B., & Carroll, E. M. (1984). Etiology of posttraumatic stress disorder in Vietnam veterans: Analysis of premilitary, military, and combat exposure influences. *Journal of Consulting and Clinical Psychology, 52,* 79–87.

Frank, E. (1984). *Treatment of depression in victims of rape.* Progress report, National Institute of Mental Health Grant No. MH29692.

Frank, E., & Anderson, B. P. (1987). Psychiatric disorders in rape victims: Past history and current symptomatology. *Comprehensive Psychiatry, 28,* 77–82.

Frank, E., Anderson, B., Stewart, B. D., Danar, C., Hughes, C., & West, D. (1988). Efficacy of cognitive behavior therapy and systemic desensitization in the treatment of rape trauma. *Behavior Therapy, 19,* 403–420.

Frank, E., & Stewart, B. D. (1983). Treatment of depressed rape victims: An approach to stress-induced symptomatology. In P. J. Clayton & J. E. Barrett (Eds.), *Treatment of depression: Old controversies and new approaches* (pp. 307–330). New York: Raven Press.

Frank, E., & Stewart, B. D., (1984). Depressive symptoms in rape victims: A revisit. *Journal of Affective Disorders, 7,* 77–85.

Frank, E., Turner, S. M., & Duffy, B. (1979). Depressive symptoms in rape victims. *Journal of Affective Disorders, 1,* 269–277.

Frank, E., Turner, S. M., & Stewart, B. D. (1980). Initial response to rape: The impact of factors within the rape situation. *Journal of Behavioral Assessment, 2,* 39–53.

Frank, E., Turner, S. M., Stewart, B. D., Jacob, M., & West, D. (1981). Past psychiatric symptoms and the response to sexual assault. *Comprehensive Psychiatry, 22,* 479–487.

Frazier, P. A. (August, 1989). *Coping strategies among rape victims.* Paper presented at the meeting of the American Psychological Association, New Orleans, LA.

Frye, J. S., & Stockton, R. A. (1982). Discrimant analysis of posttraumatic stress disorder among a group of Vietnam veterans. *American Journal of Psychiatry, 139,* 52–56.

Geer, J. H., & Silverman, E. (1969). Treatment of a recurrent nightmare by behavior modification procedures. *Journal of Abnormal Psychology, 72,* 188–190.

Geisinger, D. L. (1969). Controlling sexual interpersonal anxieties. In J. D. Krumboltz & C. E. Thorenson (Ed.), *Behavioral counseling: Cases and techniques.* New York: Holt, Rinehart and Winston.

George, L. K., & Winfield-Laird, I. (1986). Sexual assault: Prevalence and mental health consequences. Final report, National Institute of Mental Health.

Gerardi, R. J., Blanchard, E. B., & Kolb, L. C. (1989). Ability of veterans to dissimulate a psychophysiological assessment for post-traumatic stress disorder. *Behavior Therapy, 20,* 229–243.

Gerrol, R., & Resick, P. A. (1988, November). *Sex differences in social support and recovery from victimization.* Paper presented at meeting of the Association for Advancement of Behavior Therapy, New York, NY.

Girelli, S. A., Resick, P. A., Marhoefer-Dvorak, S., & Hutter, C. K. (1986). Subjective distress and violence during rape: Their effects on long-term fear. *Victims and Violence, 1,* 35–45.

Glenn, F., & Resick, P. A. (1986, November). *Incest and domestic violence as factors predicting adjustment to victimization.* Paper presented at the Association for Advancement of Behavior Therapy, Chicago, IL.

Goyer, P., & Eddleman, H. (1984). Same sex rape of nonincarcerated men. *American Journal of Psychiatry, 141,* 576–579.

Greenberg, M. A., & Stone, A. A. (1989, August) Writing about disclosed versus undisclosed traumas: Mood and health effects. Paper presented at annual meeting of the American Psychological Association, New Orleans.

Groth, A. N., & Burgess, A. W. (1980). Male rape: Offenders and victims. *American Journal of Psychiatry, 137,* 806–810.

Hamilton, M. (1960). A rating scale for depression. *Journal of Neurology, Neurosurgery, and Psychiatry, 23,* 56–62.

Haslam, M. T. (1965). The treatment of psychogenic dyspareunia by reciprical inhibition. *British Journal of Psychiatry, 111,* 280–282.

Hathaway, S. R., & McKinley, J. C. (1941). Minnesota Multiphasic Personality Inventory: Manual for administration and scoring. New York: Psychological Corporation.

Haynes, S. N., & Mooney, D. K. (1975). Nightmares: Etiological, theoretical and behavioral treatment considerations. *The Psychological Record, 25,* 225–236.

Hersen, M. (1971). Personality characteristics of nightmare sufferers. *Journal of Nervous and Mental Disease, 153,* 27–31.

Holmstrom, L. L., & Burgess, A. W. (1979). Rape: The husband's and boyfriend's initial reactions. *The Family Coordinator, 28,* 321–330.

Hoon, E. F., Hoon, P., & Wincze, J. (1976). An inventory for the measurement of female sexual arousability. *Archives of Sexual Behavior, 5,* 291–300

Horowitz, M. (1976). *Stress response syndromes.* New York: Aronson.

Horowitz, M., Wilner, N., & Alvarez, W. (1979). Impact of event scale: A measure of subjective stress. *Psychosomatic Medicine, 41,* 209–218.

Jacobson, E. (1938). *Progressive relaxation.* Chicago: University of Chicago Press.

Janoff-Bulman, R. (1979). Characterological versus behavioral self-blame: Inquiries into depression and rape. *Journal of Personality and Social Psychology, 37,* 1798–1809.

Janoff-Bulman, R. (1982). Esteem and control bases of blame: "Adaptive" strategies for victims versus observers. *Journal of Personality, 50,* 180–192.

Kaplan, H. S. (1974). *The new sex therapy: Active treatment of sexual dysfunction.* New York: Brunner/Mazel.

Kaszniak, A. W., Nussbaum, P. D., Berren, M. R., & Santiago, J. (1988). Amnesia as a consequence of male rape: A case report. *Journal of Abnormal Psychology, 97,* 100–104.

Katz, B. L., & Burt, M. R. (1988). Self-blame in recovery from rape: Help or hindrance. In A. W. Burgess (Ed.), *Rape and sexual assault* (Vol. 2). New York: Garland Publishing.

Katz, S., & Mazur, M. A. (1979). *Understanding the rape victim: A synthesis of research findings.* New York: John Wiley & Sons.

Kaufman, A., Divasto, P., Jackson, R. Voorhees, D., & Christy, J. (1980). Male rape victims: Noninstitutionalized assault. *American Journal of Psychiatry, 137,* 221–223.

Keane, T. M. (1988, November). *Trauma: A behavioral approach to assessment and treatment.* Workshop presented at meeting of the Association for Advancement of Behavior Therapy, New York, NY.

Keane, T. M., Fairbank, J. A., Caddell, J. M., & Zimering, R. T. (1989). Implosive (flooding) therapy reduces symptom of PTSD in Vietnam combat veterans. *Behavior Therapy, 20,* 245–260.

Keane, T. M., Malloy, P. F., & Fairbank, J. A. (1984). The empirical development of an MMPI subscale for the assessment of combat-related post-traumatic stress disorder. *Journal of Consulting and Clinical Psychology, 52,* 888–891.

Keane, T. M., Zimering, R. T., & Caddell, J. M. (1985). A behavioral formulation of post-traumatic stress disorder in Vietnam veterans. *The Behavior Therapist, 8,* 9–12.

Kegel, A. H. (1952). Sexual functions of the pubococcygeus muscle. *Western Journal of Surgery, 60,* 521–524.

Kilpatrick, D. G. (1984). *Treatment of fear and anxiety in victims of rape.* Final report, National Institute of Mental Health Grant No. MH29602.

Kilpatrick, D. G. (1988). Rape aftermath symptom test. In M. Hersen & A. S. Bellack (Eds.) *Dictionary of Behavioral Assessment Techniques.* Elmsford, NY: Pergamon Press, 366–367.

Kilpatrick, D. G., & Amick, A. E. (1985). Rape trauma. In M. Hersen & C. Last (Eds.), *Behavior therapy casebook* (pp. 86–103). New York: Springer Publishing Company.

Kilpatrick, D. G., & Best, C. L. (1990, April). Sexual assault victims: Data from a random national probability sample. Paper presented at the meeting of the Southeastern Psychological Association, Atlanta.

Kilpatrick, D. G., Best, C., Amick-McMullen, A., Saunders, B. E., Sturgis, E., Resnick, H., & Veronen, L. (1989, November). Criminal victimization, post-traumatic stress disorder and substance abuse: A Prospective study. Washington, DC: Association for Advancement of Behavior Therapy.

Kilpatrick, D. G., Best, C. L., Saunders, B. E., & Veronen, L. J. (January, 1987). *Rape in marriage and dating relationships: How bad are they for mental health?* Paper presented to the New York Academy of Sciences, New York, NY.

Kilpatrick, D. G., Best, C. L., Veronen, L. J., Amick, A. E., Villeponteaux, L. A., & Ruff, G. A. (1985). Mental health correlates of criminal victimization: A random community survey: *Journal of Consulting and Clinical Psychology, 53,* 866–873.

Kilpatrick, D. G., & Calhoun, K. S. (1988). Early behavioral treatment for rape trauma: Efficacy or artifact. *Behavior Therapy, 19,* 421–428.

Kilpatrick, D. G., Saunders, B. E., Amick-McMullan, A., Best, C. L., Veronen, L. J., & Resnick, H. S. (1989). Victim and crime factors associated with the development of crime-related post-traumatic stress disorder. *Behavior Therapy, 20,* 199–214.

Kilpatrick, D. G., & Veronen, L. J. (1983). Treatment of rape-related problems: Crisis intervention is not enough. In L. H. Cohen, W. L. Claiborn, & G. A. Specker (Eds.), *Crisis intervention (pp. 165–185). New York: Human Sciences Press.*

Kilpatrick, D. G., Veronen, L. J., & Best, C. L. (1985). Factors predicting psychological distress among rape victims. In C. R. Figley (Ed.), *Trauma and its wake* (pp. 113–141). New York: Brunner/Mazel.

Kilpatrick, D. G., Veronen, L. J., & Resick, P. A. (1982). Psychological sequelae to rape: Assessment and treatment strategies. In D. M. Doleys, R. L. Meredith, & A. R. Ciminero (Eds.), *Behavioral medicine: Assessment and treatment strategies* (pp. 473–498). New York: Plenum Publishing Corp.

Kilpatrick, D. G., Veronen, L. J., Saunders, B. E., Best, C. L., Amick-McMullen, A. E., & Paduhovich, J. (1987, March). *The psychological impact of crime: A study of randomly surveyed crime victims.* Final report, National Institute of Justice Grant No. 84-IJ-CX-0039.

Kimmel, D., & Van Der Veen, F. (1974). Factors of marital adjustment in Locke's Marital Adjustment Test. *Journal of Marriage and the Family, 2,* 57–63.

Koss, M. P. (1985). The hidden rape victim: Personality, attitudinal and situational characteristics. *Psychology of Women Quarterly, 9,* 193–212.

Koss, M. P. (1988, August). *Criminal victimization among women: Impact on health status and medical services usage.* Paper presented at the American Psychological Association, Atlanta, GA.

Koss, M. P., & Harvey, M. (1987). *The rape victim: Clinical and community approaches to treatment.* Lexington, MA: Stephen Greene Press.

Koss, M. P., & Oros, C. J. (1982). The sexual experiences survey: A research instrument investigating sexual aggression and victimization. *Journal of Consulting and Clinical Psychology, 50,* 455–457.

Kosten, T. R., Mason, J. W., Giller, E. L., Ostroff, R., & Harkness, L. (1987). Sustained urinary norepinephrine and epinephrine elevation in post-traumatic stress disorder. *Psychoneuroendocrinology, 12,* 13–20.

Kozak, M. J., Foa, E. B., Olasov-Rothbaum, B. & Murdock, T. (1988, September). *Psychophysiological responses of rape victims during imagery of rape and neutral scenes.* World Congress of Behavior Therapy Meeting, Edinburgh, Scotland.

Krystal, J. H., Kosten, T. R., Southwick, S., Mason, J. W., Perry, B. D., & Giller, E. L. (1989). Neurobiological aspects of PTSD: Review of clinical and preclinical studies. *Behavior Therapy, 20,* 177–198.

Lang, P. J. (1968). Fear reduction and fear behavior: Problems in treating a construct. *Research in Psychotherapy, 3,* 9–102.

Lang, P. J. (1979). A bio-informational theory of emotional imagery. *Psychophysiology, 16,* 495–512.

Lange, A. J., & Jakubowski, P. (1976). *Responsible assertive behavior.* Champaign, IL: Research Press.

Lazarus, A. A. (1966). Behavioral rehearsal vs. non-directive therapy vs. advice in effecting behavior change. *Behaviour Research and Therapy, 4,* 209–212.

Leiblum, S. R., & Pervin, L. A. (1980). *Principles and practice of sex therapy.* New York: Guilford Publications.

Litz, B. T., Blake, D. D., Gerardi, R. G., & Keane, T. M. (1990). Decision-making guidelines for the use of direct therapeutic exposure in the treatment of post-traumatic stress disorder. *The Behavior Therapist 13,* 91–93.

Lobitz, W., & LoPiccolo, J. (1972). New methods in the behavior treatment of sexual dysfunctions. *Journal of Behavior Therapy and Experimental Psychiatry, 3,* 266–271.

Masters, W., & Johnson, V. E. (1970). *Human Sexual Inadequacy.* Boston: Little, Borwn & Co.

McCahill, T. W., Meyer, L. C., & Fischman, A. M. (1979). *The aftermath of rape.* Lexington, MA: D. C. Heath.

McNair, D., Lorr, M., & Droppleman, L. (1971). *Manual, Profile of Mood States.* San Diego, CA: Educational and Industrial Testing Service.

Meichenbaum, D. H. (1974). *Therapist manual for cognitive behavior modification.* Unpublished manuscript, University of Waterloo, Ontario, Canada.

Meichenbaum, D. H. (1985). *Stress inoculation training.* Elmsford, NY: Pergamon Press.

Meyer, C. B., & Taylor, S. E. (1986). Adjustment to rape. *Journal of Personality and Social Psychology, 50,* 1226–1234.

Meyer, V., & Chesser, E. S. (1970). Behaviour therapy in clinical psychiatry. Middlesex: Penguin Books.

Miller, W. R., & Williams, A. M. (1984). Marital and sexual dysfunction following rape: Identification and treatment. In I. R. Stuart & J. G. Green (Eds.), *Victims of sexual aggression* (pp. 197–210). New York: Van Nostrand Reinhold.

Miller, W. R., Williams, A. M., & Bernstein, M. H. (1982). The effects of rape on marital and sexual adjustment. *American Journal of Family Therapy, 10,* 51–58.

Morelli, P. H. (March, 1981). *Comparison of the psychological recovery of black and white victims of rape.* Paper presented at the meeting of the Association for Women in Psychology, Boston, MA.

Mowrer, O. H. (1960). *Learning theory and behavior.* New York: Wiley.

Norris, J., & Feldman-Summers, S. (1981). Factors related to the psychological impacts of rape on the victim. *Journal of Abnormal Psychology, 90,* 562–567.

Notman, M. T., & Nadelson, C. C. (1976). The rape victim: Psychodynamic considerations. *American Journal of Psychology, 133,* 408–413.

Obler, M. (1973). Systematic desensitization in sexual disorders. *Journal of Behavior Therapy and Experimental Psychiatry, 4,* 93–101.

Orlando, J. A., & Koss, M. P. (1983). The effect of sexual victimization on sexual satisfaction: A study of the negative-association hypothesis. *Journal of Abnormal Psychology, 92,* 104–106.

Pennebaker, J. W., & Beall, S. K. (1986). Confronting a traumatic event: Toward an understanding of inhibition and disease. *Journal of Abnormal Psychology, 95,* 274–281.

Pervin, L. A., & Leiblum, S. R. (1980). Conclusion: Overview of some critical issue in the evaluation and treatment of sexual dysfunctions. In S. Leiblum & L. Pervin (Eds.), *Principles and practice of sex therapy* (pp. 377–394). New York: Guilford Publications.

Phelps, L., Wallace, D., & Waigandt, A. (1989, August). *Impact of sexual assault: Post assault behavior and health status.* Paper presented at the meeting of the American Psychological Association, New Orleans, LA.

Queen's Bench Foundation. (1976). *Rape victimization study.* San Francisco: Author.

Resick, P. A. (1987, November) The effects of age and marital status on recovery from the trauma of crime. Paper presented at the Association for Advancement of Behavior Therapy, Boston.

Resick, P. A., Calhoun, K. S., Atkeson, B. M., & Ellis, E. M. (1981). Social adjustment in victims of sexual assault. *Journal of Consulting and Clinical Psychology, 49,* 705–712.

Resick, P. A. (1981, March). *Family support to victims of rape: An intervening variable for recovery?* Paper presented at the meeting of the Association for Women in Psychology, Boston, MA.

Resick, P. A., Jordan, C. G., Girelli, S. A., Hutter, C. K., & Marhoefer-Dvorak, S. (1988). A comparative outcome study of behavioral group therapy for sexual assault victims. *Behavior Therapy, 19,* 385–401.

Resick, P. A., Veronen, L. J., Calhoun, K. S., Kilpatrick, D. G., & Atkeson, B. M. (1986). Assessment of fear reactions in sexual assault victims: A factor analytic study of the Veronen-Kilpatrick Modified Fear Survey. *Behavioral Assessment, 8,* 271–283.

Robins, L. N., Helzer, J. D., Croughan, J., and Ratcliff, K. S. (1981). The National Institute of Mental Health diagnostic interview schedule: Its history, characteristics and validity. *Archives of General Psychiatry, 38,* 381–389.

Rosenberg, M. (1965). *Society and the Adolescent self image.* Princeton, NJ: Princeton University Press.

Roth, S., Dye, E., & Lebowitz, L. (1988). Group therapy for sexual-assault victims. *Psychotherapy, 25,* 82–93.

Roth, S., & Lebowitz, L. (1988). The meaning of sexual trauma. *Journal of Traumatic Stress, 2,* 202–212.

Rothbaum, B. O., & Foa, E. B. (1988, September). Treatments of post-traumatic stress disorder in rape victims. Paper presented at the World Congress of Behaviour Therapy, Edinburgh, Scotland.

Ruch, L. O., & Chandler, S. M. (1983). Sexual assault trauma during the acute phase: An exploratory model and multivariate analysis. *Journal of Health and Social behavior, 24,* 174–185.

Ruch, L. O., Chandler, S. M., & Harter, R. A. (1980). Life change and rape impact. *Journal of Health and Social Behavior, 21,* 248–260.

Ruch, L. O., & Leon, J. J. (1983). Sexual assault trauma and trauma change. *Women and Health, 8,* 5–21.

Ruch, L. O., & Leon, J. J. (1986). The victim of rape and the role of life change, coping, and social support during the rape trauma syndrome. In S. E. Hobfoll (Ed.), *Stress, social support, and women* (pp. 137–152). New York: Hemisphere.

Russell, D. E. H. (1982). *Rape in marriage.* New York: Macmillan.

Rychtarik, R. G., Silverman, W. K., Van Landingham, W. P., & Prue, D. M. (1984). Treatment of a incest victim with implosive therapy: A case study. *Behavior Therapy, 15,* 410–420.

Sales, E., Baum, M., & Shore, B. (1984). Victim readjustment following assault. *Journal of Social Issues, 40,* 117–136.

Santiago, J. M., McCall-Perez, F., Gorcey, M., & Beigel, A. (1985). Long-term psychological effects of rape in 35 rape victims. *American Journal of Psychiatry, 142,* 1338–1340.

Saunders, B. E., Kilpatrick, D. G., Resnick, H. S., & Tidwell, R. P. (1989). Brief screening for lifetime history of criminal victimization at mental health intake. *Journal of Interpersonal Violence, 4,* 267–277.

Saunders, B. E., Mandoki, K. A., & Kilpatrick, D. G. (in press). Development of a crime-related post-traumatic stress disorder scale within the Symptom Checklist 90 Revised. *Journal of Traumatic Stress.*

Silverman, D. (1977). First do no more harm: Female rape victims and the male counselor. *American Journal of Orthopsychiatry, 47* 91–96.

Silverman, F., & Geer, J. M. (1968). The elimination of a recurrent nightmare by desensitization of a related phobia. *Behaviour Research and Therapy, 6,* 109–111.

Sorenson, S. B., Stein, J. A., Siegel, J. M., Golding, J. M., & Burnam, M. A. (1987). The prevalence of adult sexual assault: The Los Angeles Epidemiological Catchment Area Project. *American Journal of Epidemiology, 126,* 1154–1164.

Spiegel, D. (1984). Multiple personality as a post-traumatic stress disorder. In B. C. Braun (Ed.) *Psychiatric clinics of North America: multiple personality,* Vol. 7. Philadelphia, P.A.: Saunders. pp. 101–110.

Spielberger, C. D., Gorsuch, R. L., & Lushene, R. E. (1970). *The state-trait anxiety inventory.* Palo Alto, CA: Consulting Psychologists Press.

Spitzer, R. L., Williams, J. B. W., Gibbon, M., & First, M. B. (1988). *Structural clinical interview for DSM-III-R.* Washington, DC: American Psychiatric Press.

Steketee, G., & Foa, E. B. (1987). Rape victims: Post-traumatic stress responses and their treatment. *Journal of Anxiety Disorders, 1,* 69–86.

Sutherland, S., & Scherl, D. J. (1970). Patterns of response among victims of rape. *American Journal of Orthopsychiatry, 80,* 503–511.

Thorpe, J., Schmidt, E., & Costell, D. (1963). A comparison of positive and negative (aversive) conditioning in the treatment of homosexuality. *Behaviour Research and Therapy, 1,* 357–362.

Turner, S. M. (1979, December). Systematic desensitization of fears and anxiety in rape victims. Paper presented at the meeting of the Association for Advancement of Behavior Therapy, San Francisco.

Van der Kolk, B., Greenberg, M., Boyd, H., & Krystal, J. (1985). Inescapable shock, neurotransmitters, and addiction to trauma: Toward a psychobiology of post-traumatic stress. *Biological Psychiatry, 20,* 314–325.

Veronen, L., & Best, C. (1983). Assessment and treatment of fear and anxiety in rape victims. *The Clinical Psychologist, 6,* 99–101.

Veronen, L. J., & Kilpatrick, D. G. (1980a). *The response to rape: The impact of rape on self-esteem.* Paper presented at the meeting of the Southwestern Psychological Association, Oklahoma City, OK.

Veronen, L. J., & Kilpatrick, D. G. (1980b). Self-reported fears of rape victims: A preliminary investigation. *Behavior Modification, 4,* 383–396.

Veronen, L. J., & Kilpatrick, D. G. (1983). Stress management for rape victims. In D. Meichenbaum & M. E. Jaremko (Eds.) *Stress reduction and prevention.* pp. 341–374. New York: Plenum.

Veronen, L. J., Saunders, B. E., & Resnick, H. S. (November, 1988). *Partner reactions to rape.* Paper presented at the meeting of the Association for the Advancement of Behavior Therapy, New York, NY.

Weingourt, R. (1985). Wife rape: Barriers to identification and treatment. *American Journal of Psychotherapy, 39,* 187–192.

Weissman, M. M., & Bothwell, S. (1976). Assessment of social adjustment by patient self-report. *Archives of General Psychiatry, 33,* 1111–1115.

Wirtz, P. W., & Harrell, A. V. (1987). Victim and crime characteristics, coping responses, and short- and long-term recovery from victimization. *Journal of Consulting and Clinical Psychology, 55,* 866–871.

Wolfe, J., Keane, T. M., Lyons, J. A., & Gerardi, R. J. (1987). Current trends and issues in the assessment of combat-related post-traumatic stress disorder. *The Behavior Therapist, 10,* 27–32.

Wolff, R. (1977). Systematic desensitization and negative practice to alter the aftereffects of a rape attempt. *Journal of Behavior Therapy and Experimental Psychiatry, 8,* 423–425.

Wolpe, J. (1958). *Psychotherapy by reciprocal inhibition.* Stanford CA: Stanford University Press.

Wolpe, J., & Lang, P. J. (1964). A fear survey schedule for use in behavior therapy. *Behaviour Research and Therapy, 2,* 27–30.

Wolpe, J., & Lazarus, A. A. (1966). *Behavior therapy techniques: A guide to the treatment of neuroses.* Elmsford, NY: Pergamon Press.

Wooden, W. S., & Parker, J. (1982). *Men behind bars: Sexual exploitation in prison.* New York: Plenum Publishing.

Wortman, C. B. (1983). Coping with victimization: Conclusions and implications for future research. *Journal of Social Issues, 39,* 195–221.

Appendix

Semistructured Interview

Demographic Information

_____ 1. Age

_____ 2. Marital status

_____ 3. Number of children

_____ 4. Which best describes your employment in the past year?

    a. worked full time most of the year

    b. worked part time most of the year

    c. was unemployed most of the year

    d. was employed episodically

_____ 5. If you were working, what did you do?

_____ 6. How far did you go in school?

_____ 7. With whom do you live?

_____ 8. How many times have you moved? Were moves assault related? How?

Except for questions specific to postrape changes, the following questions should assess functioning both before and since the assault, whenever possible.

Social Adjustment

Question: I'd like to know what you're like when you're with other people. Could you tell me what your social life is like? How would you describe your personality? How do others see you? Would you describe yourself as an outgoing person? friendly and sociable? shy? quiet? a loner?

_____ 9. Do you have difficulty making friends?

_____ 10. Do you find it hard to talk to people you don't know very well? How do you react to new situations where you don't know people?

_____ 11. How many people do you feel you could confide in? How many really close friends do you have?

_____ 12. How well have you gotten along with your parents?

_____ 13. How have you gotten along with your spouse or the person you live with?

_____ 14. How often do you and your mother have serious arguments or fights? (Serious enough that you consider separating, or that it changes how you feel about each other for some time afterward?)

_____ 15. Have you and your mate separated (for a week or more) or been involved with police due to fighting, or sought marriage counseling?

_____ 16. If not married or cohabiting, are you dating anyone?

_____ 17. How well have you been doing in your work or school?

_____ 18. Have there been changes in your work or school status since the assault?

_____ 19. Do you feel you have lost any friends, or had any severe breaches in a close friendship as a result of the assault?

_____ 20. How many people have you confided in about the assault? What was their reaction?

_____ 21. If you have children, have they been affected by the assault? Describe:
_____

_____ 22. Has your marital status changed? Are you now divorced or separated? Have you gotten married or become engaged?

_____ 23. If now separated or divorced, do you feel this was a result of the assault?

_____ 24. Have you stopped dating anyone as a direct result of conflicts over the assault? If so, describe: _____

Sexual Adjustment

_____ 25. Do you regularly have sex with someone right now?

_____ 26. If you are not active sexually, have you been interested in sex—as measured by thoughts, fantasies, erotic dreams, etc.?

_____ 27. How regularly do you have sexual intercourse?

_____ 28. Have you had sex less often or stopped altogether as a direct result of the assault?

_____ 29. How much of the time do you enjoy sex?

_____ 30. How often are you orgasmic in sex with a partner? (by whatever means)

_____ 31. Have you had problems with painful intercourse?

_____ 32. How much did this problem interfere with your enjoyment of sex?

_____ 33. Have you had any problems with not being interested in sex? (not being turned on, not wanting sex, taking an unusually long time reaching orgasm, not having orgasms, etc.)

_____ 34. Have you had problems with vaginal infections, cervical infections, endometriosis, ovarian cysts, tumors, fibroids, etc.? Specify: _____

_____ 35. Have you experienced any unusual or frightening feelings during sex since the rape? (Examples: sees lover as rapist in darkened room, anxiety reaction to lover lying on top of her, etc.)

Previous Traumatic Experiences

_____ 36. Have you ever been robbed on the street or at home while you were there?

_____ 37. Were you ever beaten as a child? (criteria: visible physical injury) By whom?

_____ 38. Have you been beaten as an adult? By whom?

_____ 39. As a child, did anyone older than you try to get you to have some kind of sexual contact with him or her? What?

_____ 40. How many times did each act occur?

_____ 41. How old were you when this occurred?

_____ 42. Who else was involved?

_____ 43. How much force or coercion was involved?

_____ 44. As an adult (since age 15), have you ever been sexually assaulted or raped? (prior to this assault)

_____ 45. How many times did each act occur?

_____ 46. How old were you when this happened?

_____ 47. What problems did you develop as a result of this? (loss of time from work, loss of a relationship, depression, hang-up about sex, etc.)

Physical Health

_____ 48. How would you describe your current state of health over the past year? Have there been changes since the assault?

_____ 49. Have you received any medical treatment for assault-related injuries, etc.? (e.g., VD, pregnancy)

_____ 50. How many times have you been to see a doctor in the past year for other than a physical, prenatal exam, or routine test?

_____ 51. Have any of the following serious life crises happened to you recently (in the past year)?
    _____ a. surgery
    _____ b. serious illness, injury, or accident
    _____ c. death of a family member or close friend (include cousins, uncles, etc. only if close family member) Cause of death?
    _____ d. surgery of family member or close friend
    _____ e. serious illness or accident of family member or close friend
    _____ f. sexual assault of family member or close friend
    _____ g. sudden loss of a job (due to being fired or laid off)
    _____ h. loss of home due to fire or disaster
    _____ i. loss of car due to fire, disaster, or theft
    _____ j. burglary of home
    _____ k. loss of loved one through divorce, or breakup of serious relationship
    _____ l. loved one or very close friend leaving town
    _____ m. moved from one city to another
    _____ n. other

Alcohol and Drug Use

_____ 52. How often do you drink?

_____ 53. How much do you drink at a time, on the average?

_____ 54. Has drinking interfered with your work or school?

_____ 55. Has drinking interfered with relationships?

_____ 56. Do you smoke marijuana? If so, how often?

_____ 57. Have you used the following drugs? How often?
    _____ a. speed (amphetamines)
    _____ b. downers (barbituates, methaqualone)
    _____ c. cocaine
    _____ d. hallucinogens
    _____ e. opiates (heroin, morphine, opium)
    _____ f. other _____

_____ 58. How much has drug use interfered with your work and/or relationships?

Psychological History and Functioning

_____ 59. Do you have any strong or unusual fears? Fears of things that you know are not really harmful or dangerous? Fears that don't seem reasonable? (Any rape-induced fears?)

_____ 60. How disruptive are these? How much do they get in the way of your daily life?

_____ 61. Have you had any anxiety attacks? This is when you're so scared your heart pounds, your knees feel weak, your stomach feels queasy, your palms are sweaty, and you feel like you're going to fall apart. How often? (Are they rape related?)

_____ 62. Have you repeated unpleasant thoughts (more than once a day) that you couldn't stop? These are like a series of words, or a sentence, or a jingle that keeps going through your head over and over, and you don't want to think this thought but you can't help it.

_____ 63. Have you found yourself going through an activity which you repeated over and over again and couldn't stop doing? (like checking electrical appliances over and over again, handwashing over and over and still worrying if you got all the dirt off) How often?

_____ 64. Have you had thoughts that other people were against you, that they had it in for you, that you shouldn't trust anyone? Describe: _____

_____ 65. If so, how long have you felt this way?

_____ 66. How often do you feel angry at the world or get preoccupied with thoughts of revenge against someone? Do you have any violent thoughts or fantasies about the assailant? If so, would you ever act on them?

_____ 67. What are these thoughts like? Do you act on them?

_____ 68. How much have these angry feelings disrupted your day-to-day activities?

_____ 69. Have you been so depressed that it interfered with your life? How often?

_____ 70. If yes, how long did the depression last, on the average?

_____ 71. How long ago did the most recent depression occur?

_____ 72. How disruptive was the worst episode of depression? What symptoms did you have? How were your day-to-day activities different from the usual pattern?

Author Index

137

Subject Index

About the Authors

Karen S. Calhoun is Professor of Psychology and Director of Clinical Training at the University of Georgia. She is past president of the Southeastern Psychological Association. She has published a number of articles on the psychological adjustment of rape victims over time and is coeditor of several books on behavioral assessment and treatment.

Beverly M. Atkeson is a psychologist at the Regional Multidisciplinary Evaluation and Consulting Center at Florida State University. She received her Ph.D. from the University of Georgia in 1975. While working on her doctorate, she was a member of the Athens' Rape Crisis Line, serving as a crisis line counselor and presenting lectures and workshops on rape prevention and crisis intervention. Dr. Atkeson has authored several papers and articles in the area of sexual assault.

In 1977, Drs. Calhoun and Atkeson were awarded a grant from the NIMH National Center for the Prevention and Control of Rape for a longitudinal study examining depressive reactions in victims of rape.

Psychology Practitioner Guidebooks

Editors
Arnold P. Goldstein, Syracuse University
Leonard Krasner, Stanford University & SUNY at Stony Brook
Sol L. Garfield, Washington University in St. Louis

William L. Golden, E. Thomas Dowd & Fred Friedberg—
HYPNOTHERAPY: A Modern Approach

Patricia Lacks—BEHAVIORAL TREATMENT FOR PERSISTENT INSOMNIA

Arnold P. Goldstein & Harold Keller—AGGRESSIVE BEHAVIOR:
Assessment and Intervention

C. Eugene Walker, Barbara L. Bonner & Keith L. Kaufman—
THE PHYSICALLY AND SEXUALLY ABUSED CHILD: Evaluation
and Treatment

Robert E. Becker, Richard G. Heimberg & Alan S. Bellack—SOCIAL
SKILLS TRAINING TREATMENT FOR DEPRESSION

Richard F. Dangel & Richard A. Polster—TEACHING CHILD
MANAGEMENT SKILLS

Albert Ellis, John F. McInerney, Raymond DiGiuseppe & Raymond Yeager—
RATIONAL-EMOTIVE THERAPY WITH ALCOHOLICS AND
SUBSTANCE ABUSERS

Johnny L. Matson & Thomas H. Ollendick—ENHANCING CHILDREN'S
SOCIAL SKILLS: Assessment and Training

Edward B. Blanchard, John E. Martin & Patricia M. Dubbert—NON-DRUG
TREATMENTS FOR ESSENTIAL HYPERTENSION

Samuel M. Turner & Deborah C. Beidel—TREATING OBSESSIVE-
COMPULSIVE DISORDER

Alice W. Pope, Susan M. McHale & W. Edward Craighead—SELF-
ESTEEM ENHANCEMENT WITH CHILDREN AND ADOLESCENTS

Jean E. Rhodes & Leonard A. Jason—PREVENTING SUBSTANCE
ABUSE AMONG CHILDREN AND ADOLESCENTS

Gerald D. Oster, Janice E. Caro, Daniel R. Eagen & Margaret A. Lillo—
ASSESSING ADOLESCENTS

Robin C. Winkler, Dirck W. Brown, Margaret van Keppel & Amy
Blanchard—CLINICAL PRACTICE IN ADOPTION

Roger Poppen—BEHAVIORAL RELAXATION TRAINING AND
ASSESSMENT

Michael D. LeBow—ADULT OBESITY THERAPY

Robert Paul Liberman, Kim T. Mueser & William J. DeRisi —SOCIAL
SKILLS TRAINING FOR PSYCHIATRIC PATIENTS

Johnny L. Matson—TREATING DEPRESSION IN CHILDREN AND
ADOLESCENTS

Sol L. Garfield—THE PRACTICE OF BRIEF PSYCHOTHERAPY

Arnold P. Goldstein, Barry Glick, Mary Jane Irwin, Claudia Pask-McCartney
& Ibrahim Rubama—REDUCING DELINQUENCY: Intervention in
the Community

Albert Ellis, Joyce L. Sichel, Raymond J. Yeager, Dominic J. DiMattia,
& Raymond DiGiuseppe—RATIONAL-EMOTIVE COUPLES THERAPY

Clive R. Hollin—COGNITIVE-BEHAVIORAL INTERVENTIONS WITH
YOUNG OFFENDERS

Margaret P. Korb, Jeffrey Gorrell & Vernon Van De Riet—GESTALT
THERAPY: Practice and Theory, Second Edition

Donald A. Williamson—ASSESSMENT OF EATING DISORDERS:
Obesity, Anorexia, and Bulimia Nervosa